Custom[...] Etiquette of the Hunting Field

With a Guide to the Language and Terms most often used in Fox Hunting

British Library Cataloguing-in-Publication Data
A catalogue record for this book is available from
the British Library

Contents

Page
No.

Customs of the Hunting Field.........1

The Customs of the Meet..............16

The Manners and Customs of the
Hunting Field – Etiquette and
Duty....................................29

The Etiquette.....................45

The Language.....................54

A Dictionary of Fox Hunting
Terms...............................62

CUSTOMS OF THE HUNTING FIELD

The recollection of that happy span of time from nine in the morning until the hour when the slightly stiffened limbs carry a body comfortably tired to the easy chair, with the decanter within reach, causes us to lament on the decline of present-day hunting. Wire, motors, fields soaked with artificial manures, the smallholders, the loss of big subscribers, the cutting down of expenses—we go over the old ground, we excel our previous and not insignificant efforts as grumblers, and our summing-up will lead to a verdict that there are but few more seasons left for hunting.

But we know subconsciously that our grumbles are largely overdone and that hunting is not dead, nor anything like it ; but the privilege of grumbling is a right not to be surrendered—least of all when the fire is blazing and the body relapses after rough doings out of doors. Hunting will last our time, and it is to be hoped, through the lives of our children; but many of the types which we knew in our younger day are missing. They are gone—most likely for ever—and with their departure there is left a hunting field less sporting, much less picturesque, and in many ways less kindly than the one we once knew.

When we look back to the types of yesterday, first in the group we see the hunting squire. Whether he was Master or not, he held that place in the Hunt with which there is nothing comparable in any other sport. The genial autocrat, the charming host, and the leading man of the countryside, who by his personality kept as much peace among his people as erring human nature would permit, and who knew what hunting meant for the well-being of the country. Very happy is the Hunt which still owns that big-hearted genial landowner who devotes a busy lifetime to the well-being of all who live in and around his kingdom of acres. When the last of his kind leaves the field we shall see the end of the little kings who governed our countryside for many centuries and who governed it passing well.

Look at the group again and you will see a face which it is nearly impossible to find in these days— the hunting parson. A knowledgable man too, this worthy cleric, for a day with hounds once or twice a week kept him more in touch with the varied crowd, from terrier man to master and squire, than stopping at home. And as he kept the human touch so the hunting parson drew more people to church than he drove from it.

And then look for the old dealer with his well-worn clothes, his boots so sadly lacking in polish, and his weather-beaten rugged face. You will find another in his place, and of very different stamp—more often than not he is as well turned out as any man in the Hunt, and his activities are less aggressive and perhaps, in consequence, less effective than those of his kind thirty years ago. How one could see the old hand working his way through the Hunt! His job was to know everything about everyone's horses, to find the want and supply the need. A word with all, from the Master to the groom riding second horse, helped in this direction, and many was the time he would pull up as he hunted through a farmstead so that he might not miss a chance of seeing a ' likely ' one. A hard worker, and perhaps the most useful man of all to know. He did not bother to bone his boots ; and did not one well-known dealer go down to fame for having said of his man that he " cleaned me 'osses and not me breeches " ? This picturesque figure has certainly left the group.

Others come to mind, and one thinks of them with affection, as we must of all pleasant recollections, and with regret at their passing. The old huntsman, a little portly and red of face, who had hunted the same pack all his life, never very smart and with the homely touch about his carriage and seat. We all felt that he well deserved his cottage and small pension for sporting services rendered. The earth-stopper on his old pony and the scarlet-coated runner—quaint figures and hardy old fellows with a knowledge profound—nearly all gone and not likely to be replaced.

And most of all must we deplore the passing of the sporting farmer, the man who loved hunting and hounds for their own sake and to whom hunting was the chief pleasure of life. There are still hunting farmers left, but the type seems to be dying out, and what is left of him is to be found in the old dog-cart. He's too old and stiff to get into a saddle now, but he is still hunting and as keen as ever.

Who fill the vacant places in the group ? First, we must certainly place the hunting lady, who in most Hunts seems to outnumber the men, for more young women than ever seem to take to hunting now, just as there are fewer young men. Then, and mostly with the Midland packs, we find the gaps filled by Americans, and we must be grateful to them, for they do much for the countryside and for hunting.

Nor must we forget that strange fellow who often goes so well, but who is hunting man to-day, racing motorist to-morrow, golfer the next day, and a devil of a handy man with a gun as well. A queer type this and generally likeable.

Hunting is in the melting pot, yet I have faith in these new people ; but will they find they are fighting a battle for the love of a sport that has become held up because of wire, motorists and smallholders, supported by that not inconsiderable unit, the anti-sport brigade ? Perhaps in large measure the pot will yield a dish richer and more promising than is expected.

As regards finance, one treads on somewhat thin ice. Although the modern custom of 'capping' non-subscribers at a meet of hounds is one that only came into force a few years before the War, it is in reality very much older than this. As Sir Moses Mainchance of the Hit 'Im and 'Old 'Im Shire remarked, " our old friend L.S.D. must occasionally be looked in the face," and to follow the track of Surtees we find that Tom Hills of the Old Surrey always capped the followers of the Hunt after a good day. And that worthy citizen, grocer, and good sportsman John Jorrocks paid with enthusiasm for himself and his attendant friend the Yorkshire man, in a five shilling piece, and then went home with his hanger-on to devour a " quarter of roast lamb ". Lucky Mr. Jorrocks ! Half a crown is the sum which we of to-day are asked to pay towards the poultry and damage fund ; if we hunt with a strange pack the Secretary will ask us to give him £2 or £3 ; and if the day be blank or scentless and we shall have paid £3 3s. for our hireling, and other odd shillings in sundry 'heart warmers ', which will bring the total cost of our day's sport up to £6 or £7. It hardly seems value for money ; but on the other hand there is no doubt that hunting cannot exist unless what Mr. Bragg termed " the raw material " is forthcoming.

So 'capping' is necessary. We may not like it

but it has come to stay, and I am given to understand that many Hunts are to tighten up their rules during the forthcoming season. Of course, the correct procedure is to write to the secretary of the Hunt and tell him that you intend to hunt with the hounds on a certain date, at the same time enclosing the necessary cheque for the cap levied by the pack for the season. But how many shirk doing this? How many try to avoid the attentions of the secretary? Verily that official must possess Argus eyes, the temperament of an archangel, and the patience of Job, not to mention on occasions the ruthlessness of a Cromwell! After all, a sport which is worth enjoying is worth paying for, and there should be no escaping of Hunt subscriptions.

A season or two back, a secretary friend of mine was accosted by a blue-stocked, be-legginged sportsman at the meet, whose horse was unclipped and whose bridle was all buckles. Said this apparition, " I have a letter here from my brother." The secretary took it and pocketed it. In the evening while changing he read the precious epistle, which ran : " Dear ——, This is my half-brother, please be good to him and show him as much sport as possible." And the writer was a *non-paying* subscriber, and, as the secretary averred, a vulpecide to boot!

There is no excuse for not paying caps, for if men or women cannot afford to do so they had better stay at home, rather than cause the secretary of the Hunt, the Master, and incidentally themselves, needless embarrassment. One does not go and shoot with a friend and then try to slink away without remunerating his keepers. Those who try to escape Hunt caps are in this category, and bring discredit to fox-hunting. Of course, exceptions can be, and very often are, made. For example, adjoining Hunts

THE DUKE OF BEAUFORT'S HOUNDS

6

do not usually cap the members of a particular pack for the same amount as strangers; in some cases they are allowed three free days. Nor should any cap be levied on children under sixteen years of age, for these are the horsemen and women of the future, and as a tentative suggestion I would say that those parties who come from riding schools in the vicinity of the Hunt might well be let off with half or even a quarter of the usual cap, for they generally only ride to the meet and go home again. What matter if they do see the first fox found? Surely such a proceeding will give them keenness and a longing for more. Here then are embryo subscribers to the Hunt funds.

On this question of Hunt finance let me say that many Hunt subscriptions are levied in the wrong manner. Let me take a country I know well, where the minimum subscription is the same for one as for four days—obviously unfair on the man or woman who has only the time or means to hunt one day a week. No matter if, as I have been told, three out of the four are woodland days. Some people prefer that kind of hunting. But should no one come out on those days, why go to the expense of preserving and hunting foxes in that part of the country?

Another case comes to my notice of a man with one horse who lives on the outskirts of three Hunts, out of which he can just get one day a week—with one pack, not each. Obviously, £10 from him to each of the three packs would be a fair amount, *i.e.* £30 for a day a week—whereas, if he gives the subscription demanded to each, it totals £75.

In another country two gentlemen—farmers, each occupying and farming their own land—one of them over 500 acres, and each with a celebrated covert in the midst—are expected to subscribe the same amount as those whose land occupation stops at the ground their house and stables are built on, with perhaps the addition of a tennis court and kitchen garden. The result is that neither of them comes out at all. This does not help fox-hunting.

Surely the time has come for the hunting farmer to contribute a little bit towards his sport, even though he is the occupier of land over which hounds hunt. The non-hunting farmer has to bear the same brunt without the fun, whereas the hunting farmer has the chance of coming into direct contact with the members of the Hunt, who may buy some old hay or oats from him, if, as is very seldom, he has any to offer, or if he has a well-bred, well-mannered young horse, which is still more seldom. The latter gets all his schooling with hounds.

I do not suggest that a cash subscription should be demanded, but I do think that at the present low price of forage a couple of loads of hay or straw, a few sacks of oats or beans, say up to £5, would not be felt. A couple of Hunt horses might be summered at grass, or if the man be a dairy farmer living near the kennel, a few gallons of milk for the bitches and whelps would be welcomed. All these things have to be bought by the Master through the middleman, and some sort of scheme like this would help the balance-sheet. I know that many Hunts pride themselves on the large number of farmers who hunt. My personal experience is that the non-hunting farmer is the backbone of the Hunt, and if it is on good terms with him, all is well with it. I think it fair to mention one subscription list that is a model of fairness, and that is the Badminton. Every class of subscriber, and his status in the country, is taken into account, and allowed for accordingly.

I know I shall not be in agreement with some, but

I see no reason for any rebate on the Army, medical, or veterinary professions. The former are in a good deal better position for hunting and polo than their civilian brethren nowadays, and the two latter can combine a good deal of business with pleasure, even if they may miss a gallop sometimes.

The subscriptions paid by livery stable keepers and dealers is often ridiculously inadequate to the amount of hunting and trade done in the hunting field, a couple of subscriptions often doing duty for eight or ten. This is manifestly unfair. In addition, one might charge every riding school party just the same amount, which I have shown is the wrong attitude to adopt to those who would help the cause of fox-hunting. Surely everyone, even motorists, can afford to contribute a small sum such as 5*s.* or 10*s.* per day with hounds ? One spends much more than this at the theatre or at supper after the play for not half the interest and the amusement and the thrills which fox-hunting may and can bring.

Despite these facts of finance, hunting after all continues ; there still are a certain number of people with money to keep " the tambourine a'rowling ". Even if there was none of this wealth it is questionable indeed if hunting would altogether perish, for we can hardly visualize the heather-clad dales of Yorkshire or the rock-strewn fells of Cumberland, or the downs and pastures of the South without a pack of hounds somewhere in the neighbourhood.

Before wire had made such an increase, there was more money to lubricate the wheels ; poultry claims had not advanced to the scale they have now, when every bird taken by a fox is a pedigree prize-winner whose loss can only be assuaged by heavy monetary compensation.

When it costs nearly £15,000 a year to hunt one

of the Shire packs, when everything is treble the cost, three-quarters of every pound goes to pay rates and taxes and death duties, then surely the time has come to make judicious use of the pruning knife. No useful purpose can be served by giving up Hunt balls or Point-to-Points, or even adopting the expedient of the Irish M.F.H., whose economies consisted of putting his men into brown breeches instead of white ! Even so, many packs would do a great deal better if they had a Master of the character of Flurry Knox—he who " looked liked a gentleman among stable boys, and a stable boy among gentlemen ", for did he not impress upon the foolish and fatuous Major Sinclair Yeates that he should never give more than " half a crown for a donkey because there was no meat on them ? "

Probably in the next decade we shall see very few solo-Masterships. Packs will be ruled by a committee, with one person acting on their behalf, with a gentleman huntsman, and probably at least one amateur whipper-in.

It is a question, of course, whether joint-Masterships are really beneficial to hunting ; but in a period when the position calls for drastic measures, nothing else remains to be done. And I think that, for the next decade at least, Masterships will become shorter and shorter ; for even the short term of two seasons in command of a four-days-a-week pack is a heavy drain on the pocket.

Even when a Master's guarantee has been paid there always remains a large debit balance for the Master himself to settle. So when we take this into consideration, we realize that a Master of Foxhounds' life of the present day is certainly not a bed of roses ; for his post-bag is a heavy one, his ears are permanently assailed with clamours for settlement of poultry bills, damages, and the irate comments of country dwellers whose pedigree poultry-yards have been decimated, whose stock have suffered through hounds running over the land.

And then there is no doubt that we shall see countries—as the York and Ainsty, the Middleton and the Holderness already have been—divided, and other countries amalgamated, in very much the same fashion as the Braes of Derwent and the North Durham. The consequences of this mean that many areas of country will be given up and not hunted, and in others the requirements of local housing, works, and factories will ride paramount over the chase of the fox.

If you associate hunting with a soft winter's day, green fields, and the red loam of ploughland, it does not cause you any satisfaction to realize that hounds are drawing for the fox in a district congested with villas, and that in all probability the fox has had to thread his way along arterial roads, through serried phalanx of motor-cars, whose petrol fumes have obliterated all traces of scent. You cannot associate that scene with a " forty minutes on the grass " or the " red of an English woodland, or the cry of an English pack ".

Far better that the district remained unhunted, or that its good country was utilized for drag hunting. In many countries near London draghounds will gradually take the place of foxhounds, especially with the menace of electric railways, which is more near than people imagine.

In conclusion I think that everyone should hearken unto two excellent sets of precepts which were compiled, the one in 1746 by the Lord Tankerville of the day for the benefit of those who followed the fortunes of the old Charlton Hunt (now the Cowdray), the other, much more recently, by Mr. T. J. Young, sometime Master of the Haydon in Northumberland.

Lord Tankerville wrote, perhaps with his tongue in his cheek but nevertheless in a severe and practical manner, as follows :—

The Hounds not to be kept behind the Huntsman in the Morning to what ever Country they go, except at times when they are oblig'd to go through covers.

The Whippers-in to be forward and if any Hound or more happens to prole from the Roade they goe to call on them, but to use no whip, for if they know their Names at Home they'll obey Abroad.

When you are come to your beat the Huntsman only to Speak to the Hounds and the leſs the better.

The Whippers-in to have a good look out to stop any Hounds that Steales away with a Scent and leaves the Body of the Pack behind, unleſs 'tis a good one and has time to give notive for the rest to be well laiſ in.

The Whippers-in not to speak by way of incouraging any Hounds in Cover, but in case of Riot they shall *gently* rate them off.

Aſ soon as they have found, one Whipper-in to go with the Huntsman, the other to stay behind to bring any stragling or tale hounds that may be left behind, which will seldom happen if the tow Boyes knows their Busineſs and dos their duty.

'Tis not a part of the busineſs of a Whipper in at any time to speak to a hounds otherwise then together, or rate into the Huntsman who sh'ud always be with the Main Body of the Hounds.

Nither Huntsman or Boys to Speake to the hounds while running with a good scent. On a midleing one the Huntsman to incourage his Hounds at discretion, without any other persons interfereing.

The Company always at a distance that the hounds may not be hurryed, which is the loſs of many a fox, as well as the loſs of a great deal of Beauty a good pack of hounds will shew at a Half scent.

When the hounds from running comes to a Check, the Huntsman is not to speak but allow the Hounds have their first Caste and if after that not of the Huntsman to observe the point at which they threw up, and then to help the Hounds to the best of his Judgement, but without hurry, for when a Fox is sinking, time must be taken, as he then runs short, and is often left behind by Clapping Down.

The Gentlemen for their own sake will observe that a Confabulation down the wind often heads a Fox and indangers the whole days Sport.

At the dawn of the present century Mr. Young gave the Ten Commandments of fox-hunting to the hunting world of that time. They are still as fresh and brimful of straightforward common-sense as ever, and I believe have been quoted all over the world. Here they are *in extenso* and as they were originally penned :—

THE TEN COMMANDMENTS OF FOX-HUNTING.

Article I. Every man shall present himself at the place of meeting quietly, suitably clothed, and in good time. He who rides his hunter steadily thereto is better than he who uses a hack. He who drives tandem for display or who uses any manner of engine or machine, except as a necessity, is an abomination.

Article II. Every man shall first salute and speak words of comfort to the huntsman and whippers-in, knowing full well that they have hard work to perform. He shall then count the hounds and examine them with great joy, but in a quiet manner. He shall then likewise cheerfully salute his friends. He that shall say that the day will be a bad-scenting one, or in any manner endeavour to prophesy evil, is an abomination.

Article III. It is acceptable that those of experience shall, at all times, give explanation and encouragement by word and deed to all young persons, so that fox-hunting may continue in the land from generation to generation. He who thinks he knows, when he knows not, is an abomination.

Article IV. Every man shall remember that the ground he passes over is not his own property. Whosover uses not due care and consideration is an abomination.

Article V. He who talks loudly or who leaps unnecessarily is an abomination. He who wears an apron or mackintosh on wet days or who uses any other device for making a mountebank of himself, or who in any way causes inconvenience to any hound or hunt servant is an abomination.

Article VI. If it be possible, let every true believer abstain from all meat and drink, save only such as is necessary to sustain life. Let the whole day be kept as a special fasting and strengthening of the mind for the Chase. In the evening he shall partake of suitable meat and drink, and on the evening after a good day he shall have a special allowance.

Article VII. He who, of his own free will, goes home before the hounds do, or who is displeased with the day, or who is not fully uplifted, joyful and thankful because of the day, is an abomination.

Article VIII. Whosoever kills or takes a fox by any other means save by hunting is an abomination ; may his dwelling become desolate and his possessions a desert ; may his mind be filled with bitterness and his body with pain.

Article IX. Whosoever lives a cheerful, good neighbour, striving to help and encourage his friends at all times, and who hunts on foot if he has not a horse, and by whose behaviour the Scarlet is never brought into dishonour ; may he live long and be happy and may his possessions be as the sand by the sea-shore for multitude.

Article X. And may all men, rich and poor, have equal rights and pleasures in the Chase if they devoutly agree to these articles.

The Meet

LET us set out for the meet, then, and try our luck at this fox-hunting about which you have heard so much, in which you have longed to join, and around which so strange and such an age-long glamour has been set.

What, I wonder, is the hold which fox-hunting has on the people, whether mounted or on foot? A friend of mine, father of his remote village set in the Wiltshire downs, was walking down the street, his mind on the coming Armistice Day, the affairs of his branch of the British Legion, the gathering there in two days' time in that same street—the Silence. The oldest inhabitant met him and wished him a fine day for Monday, to which my friend said yes, he did hope the weather would be kind on Armistice Day. "Armistice Day!" replied the old man in his soft, burring voice. "Armistice Day!—Hounds be cooming to the village." For sixty years or more this old fellow had seen, when he could, the annual meet in the village street, and so that morning in November will remain the year's big day to old

William, and will continue to remain so, let us hope, for more kindly years to come.

As we ride out of the stable yard I naturally look at your horse, his saddle and bridle, and your clothes, having taken an almost impertinent part in the choosing of everything. I wouldn't have those girths too tight to start with, or that curb-chain. Why do some grooms pull up that throat lash so tight? It won't really hurt your horse, but it will irritate him, especially when he starts to sweat, as we certainly hope he will when the little red-brown rascal shows us his brush. I always think that a good-fitting bridle has an easy look— there is no appearance of tightness anywhere, no pulling of the bit up into the corners of the mouth, but it lies easily just below, all the leather lying snugly with no bulging and no stretching, the nose-band forming a level line across the nose.

You won't be feeling sad this morning, or anything approaching it, but anyone who may be feeling that way will look more so if his spurs droop down dejectedly pointing to the ground! Keep them well up your heel and parallel to the ground. Fashion says the higher the better, without much regard, by the way, to utility; but that's Fashion's way. However, it is of no great moment as spurs now are of very little practical value—if, by the way, they ever were. Button your coat up well, all three buttons, for if you don't you'll look rather like a lamp-shade—a most unpleasant thought—and set your hat on right. To wear a hunting hat at the back of the head is suggestive of that unfortunate nit-wit who is said to be found in every village. To wear it tilted over the nose will make you look like a big question mark. Anyway, jam your hat down, and if it is a little on one side you'll look none the worse, and on some of our heads we get the better grip by a slightly jaunty angle. I am sorry, by the way, but I forgot to mention hatguards. Wear one if you want to, or I should say if it is necessary, but avoid it if you can. If yours is the "hat upon the skyline" conveying to the huntsman the glad news that you have viewed a fox, you'll find you just can't stand up in your stirrups and hold your hat high at full arm stretch—unless, of course, you pull your coat up by the tab over the top of your head —a horrid thought.

What is the meaning and secret of the hold which fox-hunting has on so many people? We have all heard that it predominates among Englishmen, how typically British it is in character, and how inseparably associated, too, with the English countryside, although I would like to remark in passing that there are over one hundred recognised hunts in America. But although much of all this is true, it still does not entirely explain why man and maid go fox-hunting. I

. . . JUST CAN'T HOLD YOUR HAT AT FULL ARM
STRETCH——

wish I could explain it to you myself, and I never wished it more than on this winter's morning as you and I ride to the meet for your first day out with hounds. It certainly is not, as many people think, because of some inward and unconquerable urge to kill foxes. This is merely incidental and the only reaction which I get to a kill is whether or not hounds deserved their fox, a certain satisfaction that the farmers are rid of yet another one, and very little regret, unless he put up a stout show, for the varmint rightly called the world's thief, for whom the world has little sympathy and with whom ever-kindly Nature (but is she, by the way?) has endowed a cunning and cleverness so extraordinary as to be unique in the animal world. Shed no tears for Mr. Fox—he is amazingly well able to look after himself—but don't unduly condemn him. Nature gave him a nasty nature, and since he lives in a hard world, as does all wild life, he's not going to starve if he can help it.

No, it is not blood lust which sets us down the road this day, or the desire to be British, or to race each other over the countryside, or to find all the jumps we can, or to look pretty in scarlet. I can't tell you really, nor can anyone, but I can tell you a few things which go to make this wonderful sport, and I hope with all my heart you may share in some of them.

You will find your horse a different being in the hunting-field; more difficult, perhaps more fretful, more headstrong; but, again, as in humans when in company on an "occasion," the more attractive, and so perhaps even more lovable. You will find you are yourself a somewhat different being. More self-dependent, more understanding of your horse, more sympathetic with those who follow with you, and having kinder feelings for anyone in trouble. And you will find, too, among those who hunt with you a new companionship and have for them a greater respect. A kindly word received and given and a friendly smile makes for a warmth of friendship which will be something new to you. And as the hunts become more frequent, you will find yourself one of a little community who have acquired the great fellowship and understanding of the horse and the hunt, who think as you do, who speak a language which you will learn, who are kindly people of big understanding, and who are sportsmen in the truest and best sense of the word, for they are considerate to their horses, their servants, and those who follow them.

You will find a Nature different from her whom you knew when you strolled across the field or saw through the window of your car. A disturbed and fascinating Nature. Scurrying rabbits and funny little things darting about the woods and into the hedgerows, the woods full of the music of hounds and the crashing of horses, mud flying and swollen winter streams winding in and out through the trees. Nature in winter is really known to so few of us, and nearly all of us who do not hunt or shoot miss so much of her sombre beauty.

It is said that the danger of hunting makes it the fascinating sport which it undoubtedly is— but I wonder. No doubt the thrill of attempting something requiring that little bit of extra nerve adds spice to the hunt, but not numbering myself among the brave and fearless, I cannot personally attach too much importance to this.

And so you see we are not much nearer to discovering what this hunting really is. An idea was put into my head by a friend only the other day which may be the answer, after all, and certainly it comes nearer to an explanation than anything I can think of. The suggestion he made to me was that hunting is nothing more than a great adventure, and that because of this it makes a great appeal to men and women who are of any spirit, and as Englishmen have always been known and admired for their love of adventure, that is perhaps why fox-hunting is associated essentially with Englishmen.

For it is indeed an adventure, and where is such to be found otherwise in these days? As you and

I ride down the road together we know that as we round the bend of the road and come upon the meet we shall find the picturesque and adventurous—the hounds, the huntsman, the village green, the hospitable " George," lichen-tiled and brown with age, country folk and the regular foot followers, and we shall hear the clip-clop of horses as they step gingerly down the ramp from the motor horse-box. All is chatter and cheery greetings, perhaps even more so in the parlour of " The George." Here is a fitting dawn to adventure to come.

Hunting people figure largely in literature. They have books to themselves in large numbers, or rather, they and their horses have; and in countless novels a chapter and more is devoted to tales of the hero and heroine in the hunting-field, and of their horses' " scampering " hooves, as one well-known " best seller " authoress described them. I don't like "scampering," by the way, but never mind. What I want to tell you, however, is this, and it is important to the beginner. Don't be afraid that directly we move off from the meet you will find at every turn red-faced colonels and others with " Bateman " eyes, whose red will turn to purple as they roar, " Gad, sir! " at you. Nor will you necessarily find the too-too perfectly habited lady in immaculate topper or the elderly parchment-faced, hard-bitten dame who will look you through and through in pity and disdain.

There are few of these, but, on the other hand, there will be many to give you welcome and understanding.

While we are on the subject, don't imagine that the only people who dare to be hearty with each other are the Master and the Squire. I blame many writers for giving this false impression.

We will be at "The George" in a few moments now and see some types—and jolly ones, too—and plenty of farmers, and who are jollier on a hunting morning? A cherry brandy will do you no harm, and on an extra cold morning a cherry b *and* b is very easy drinking.

The best time to arrive at the meet depends entirely upon the distance travelled. It is a great mistake to arrive just as hounds move off, as even if you have come but a short distance your horse will be all the better for a few minutes' stand-by with loosened girths. You must never be late; it is discourteous to the Master and the hunt, though, of course, there are excuses at times for everyone. Assume we have come some two or three miles, say, as you and I have, it is as well to arrive about fifteen minutes beforehand. Time for the horses to take a breather; time for them to get accustomed to having other horses and many people around them; time for a drink and a cheery word, for good-fellowship is the essence of hunting. I have noticed at those times when circumstances have caused me to be late for a meet, and so compelled me to join the field after they have moved off, that my hunter is always more "het-up" than if he had stood by with other horses for a time.

Well, here we are, so slip off your horse, slack your girths a couple of holes, and here's one of the "regulars" anxious to hold our horses and take a drink at our expense when we have moved off. Promise me one thing now and for always: cultivate a personal acquaintance with hounds and acquire all the hound knowledge which you can. To you, hunting will become so much more interesting, and you will be the superior to many, for I am sorry to say there are some to whom the hounds are of no moment except as being incidental and, of course, essential to the chase. To you today all hounds will appear to be sufficiently alike as to be indistinguishable one from another. Later they will become individual, having names and developing characters and attributes which will mark them in your mind. So come and see them and wish the huntsman good-day as he sits his horse among them, and he'll be glad to meet you. Yes, first in importance come the pack, then the huntsman, the whippers-in, the Master and "the field." *We* are not very important really,

ONE OF THE "REGULARS."

though we may think we are—less so even than the hunt's second horsemen. Anyway, when hounds are running, as far as "the field" is concerned all are equal, whether it be His Grace or Your Grocer.

Among what is really a great number of duties, the hunt secretary has the job of "capping" non-subscribers. I dislike asking people for money, and I always feel sorry for the secretary who has to chase round among the strangers and collect the cap. This is generally done while hounds are drawing, when you may be quite sure he would sooner be watching what is afoot. To produce money from your pocket—perhaps from a note-case—when you are holding reins and whip and the wind may be blowing and the rain falling, is a nuisance to you—I have seen notes blowing about in the breeze—and it is not courteous to compel the secretary to seek you out and ask for the cap. Therefore I would extract yet another promise from you, and it is always to find the secretary before hounds move off and offer him your cap. He will appreciate this, I know.

Now for that quick one, if we can get over the threshold and fight our way through to the bar. Here are new faces to you, to become familiar as the season wears on—friendships, I am sure, in the making. This is generally the time to find out which covert we are likely to draw, for it is ten to one some old familiar among the foot followers will ask where directly we leave the door, anxious to get a start down the road. The secretary will most likely know or the most local of the farmers, or the Master will tell us, if we get the chance of a word with him. Ten minutes soon slip away, so out to our horses, up with the girths with a steady squeeze, but good and tight now, and get the horses on the move before they chill down. They're drawing Banham's Gorse first, so pull to one side to give hounds the road. Yes, here they come. "Hounds, gentlemen, please." Wait a moment. Now slip in here, and don't ride up on any horse's tail. How do you feel? Good? Come on. Big Adventure's round the corner.

THE MANNERS AND CUSTOMS OF THE HUNTING FIELD; ETIQUETTE AND DUTY TOWARDS FARMERS; DRESS, EQUIPMENT, ETC.

By Sir Charles Frederick, baronet

THE manners and customs of the present-day hunting field differ little from those that were accepted by sportsmen in the past, and it is certainly not with any desire to improve upon what has been written for the guidance of other generations that this chapter is penned. Changing conditions may absolve a writer from reference here and there to something which once seemed important, while other aspects assume more prominence and call for greater emphasis when we make our review. Relationships between the fox-hunter and farmer surely come within the category of these latter. Scrupulous consideration for those hospitable folk who place their land at his disposal has always been a first duty, but there are a number of causes to-day which combine to multiply his obligations manifold and to magnify the penalties resulting from transgression. Time was when a farmer could carry his complaint of broken fences, damaged crops, or whatever it might be, to a sympathetic landlord, himself a member of the Hunt likely enough, and highly jealous of its good name. The trouble, whatever it had been, was comfortably adjusted and no one was any the worse. If indeed the coming of rent day, with its recital of a bad harvest, along with the various ills and adversities which the agriculturist is heir to, fell upon friendly ears, one party might indeed feel himself the gainer. Fox-hunting, in short, was not without its compensations. Nowadays the average farmer either owns his land or else he farms under a landlord who frankly disclaims responsibility for third-party risks of this nature. Moreover, times are very bad. Prices are down, the cost of labour is up, and most of those good people on whose land the fox-hunter enjoys his sport find it a difficult task to balance their accounts at the end of the year. Hunt Committees certainly have extended the scope and scale of compensation to meet the new conditions, and Masters of Hounds on their part keep constant touch with the farmers and their organisations. It is none the less with the individual fox-hunter that the responsibility continues to rest. Upon his relationship with the farmers in his own neighbourhood may easily depend for better or worse their outlook upon hunting in general, while a single misdemeanour in the hunting field can bring the whole community into disrepute. Let us see what there is that we can do to minimise the damage and inconvenience which a day's hunting might result in where the visitors are ignorant or careless, or both. We can avoid at all costs riding over growing crops, seeds and beans more especially, and when such fields have to be crossed keep closely to the headland. We can and must make it our rule never to jump fences when hounds are not running, and if our horse is not capable of negotiating a normal fence without crashing through and destroying it we can ensure that he is schooled at our expense elsewhere than in the hunting field. We can use every endeavour to see that gates are not left open, more especially those that adjoin a road, foreseeing the trouble and annoyance caused to the stockowner whose animals are thus let loose. Such accidents, if they do occur, can often be smoothed over by the aid of a small present to the shepherd or stockman as some atonement for the extra work imposed. Hunting folks appear to disburse a surprising quantity of small change in the course of every day's hunting, and it seems a thousand pities that they do not spend it to greater advantage. In many countries it actually pays the loafer from the town to journey by train or otherwise to the different meets of hounds and there, posing as a " runner," to receive the largesse of the hunting man for doing precisely nothing. How much better surely if all this wasted cash went into the pockets of the hedge-cutter, the shepherd, and the various employees on the farm where the fox-hunter is privileged to disport himself! The red coat would at all events gain much in popularity and the toast of fox-hunting be honoured more frequently in the village inn.

Subscriptions.

Second only to his duty towards the people over whose land he rides comes another increasing obligation for the fox-hunter, namely, that of paying his footing in the hunting field.

Gone for ever are the happy-go-lucky days when each man was a law unto himself, giving whatever he felt disposed to as a contribution towards the Hunt which he honoured, and often parting with nothing at all. Strict and arbitrary tariffs are the order of the day, and so long as the expenses of running a hunting country continue to mount up as they do at present, one can never be certain that the call upon the subscriber's pocket represents the last word. However, there is nothing else for it but to pay up and look pleasant, finding consolation in the fact that hunting, while it is the best, remains also, in spite of the great increase in cost, the cheapest of all sports. If you doubt me put your eggs into another basket for once— let it be a grouse moor, a yacht, a salmon river or deer forest— and when you have balanced your accounts on profit and loss lines tell me whether I am right. It is better for a new arrival, whether his visit be long or short, to seek out the Hunt Secretary and proffer whatever contribution is expected of him rather than wait until he is run to earth. In terms of cash the result will be the same in either case, but in the impression created (and which of us can confess complete indifference to such considerations ?) there is all the difference in the world. The Secretary will be able, moreover, to help a newcomer in a variety of ways—information as to where stabling can be obtained or forage bought can be had for the asking and enlightenment sought on the many little items of etiquette and procedure which interest a newcomer.

Punctuality is a virtue in any fox-hunter and the lack of it something akin to a vice. Not all of us, it has been wisely said, are good enough men or sufficiently well mounted to see a fox killed at the end of a fine run, but we can all see him found if we do but take the trouble. When one thinks of all the expenditure of time and effort, and indeed of money too, that is poured into a season's hunting, it does seem the height of folly that a man should risk so much by the failure to arrive at the meet in good time. Personal considerations apart, the presence of late comers cutting about the country in pursuit of hounds is prejudicial to sport, and the Master is entitled to a strict observance of this simple formality. It will be the aim and object of all those who come out hunting to study the wishes of the latter in every respect, and to help him so far as it lies in their power. The best assistance is usually of a negative character ; that is to say, his followers can help him more effectually by the things that they refrain from doing than by the activities that they show. People who can holloa

and blow whistles, crack whips and turn hounds to the huntsman, or who supply information as to where the fox has gone
at times of crisis and emergency, are emphatically not those
who make an M.F.H.'s task easier nor do they aid him in his
efforts to show sport. The men (and women) who can be
silent, who will keep an eye on the hounds and pull up when-
ever these show signs of checking, who look where they are
going and keep off the farmers' seeds without being called
upon to do so, are those who will earn the gratitude of the
man in command. Far be it from me to suggest that a member
of the field who can supply useful information concerning the
hunted fox, should through motives of modesty withhold it.
If in doubt let him carry his tale to the Master, who will judge
whether it is worth while passing on. The huntsman, if the
information is to help him, will want to know :
(1) Where the fox was last seen.
(2) How long ago.
(3) In which direction he was going.
The last-named point may be conveyed by the direction of
one's horse's head quicker than by word of mouth.

The old maxims still hold good and, maybe, no apology is
needed for repeating them. When hounds are proceeding
from covert to covert they must take precedence and be given
ample room no less than when they are engaged in hunting a
fox. Nothing looks so bad as the spectacle of riders trampling
on the sterns of the pack or crowding round them and their
huntsman when on the road. When a fox breaks covert the
hounds that have furthest to come to the horn should not have
to thread their way through the dangers of iron-shod heels.
In the interests of sport time and room must be given so that
they may get together and settle to their work. On bad
scenting days, which unfortunately outnumber the good in
the best of seasons, the progress is necessarily slow, and the
rider must show patience and discretion, avoiding the tendency
to ride " in the huntsman's pocket," and giving him and his
hounds both time and space for manœuvre when such is
required.

The question may be asked whether young people enter the
hunting field nowadays better grounded in the necessary pre-
liminaries than their fathers or grandfathers, or whether the
reverse is the case. If the latter, it is certainly not due to any
lack of keenness on the part of those who are " joining up "
now nor for want of books of instruction written for their
benefit. They are nevertheless denied, through the altered

conditions of the times, some of the facilities for riding in the summer which would have been formerly enjoyed and they have not the invaluable experience of riding their own horse or pony to the meet and of returning home in the same fashion after hunting. It will probably be conceded, therefore, that in the matter of riding alone young people start their hunting careers with more to learn than did those who preceded them.

Gates.

Take the problem of gates, for instance. It is one that the most ambitious Thruster need not affect to despise for he will probably have to confess that on most days, and in most countries, he will require to negotiate more gates than fences in the course of the proceedings. No man, more emphatically still no woman, is competent and qualified to go out hunting until the elements of this simple practice are mastered. A man can dismount and remount at a gate if necessary and continue to do so in his passage across country without eliciting compassion, but a woman seated on a side-saddle cannot do this without difficulty and might find herself marooned in default of male assistance. When two or more people, riding abreast, arrive at a gate, the task of opening it devolves upon the person whose horse's head is opposite to the latch, while his companions rein back and follow him in single file, the nearest holding himself in readiness to move up and assist with a lift or a push if requested. Unfortunately gates in the Midlands, whatever may be the case elsewhere, do not nowadays receive from their owners the attention to which they are entitled, and it seems to be the exception rather than the rule to cross a farm where they function as their makers intended them. Where the farmer does his shepherding on horseback he can be trusted to see that his gates open and shut properly, but otherwise they are apt to be neglected, which is poor economy and bad for the life of the gate. While on the subject it may be mentioned that when hounds are running, the etiquette of the hunting field expects us to give a gate a push with our whip as we pass through so that anyone following may catch it who arrives in time to avail themselves of the chance, but it does *not* require us to check our horse or look round. Before leaving this prosaic theme it may be mentioned that one of the most frequent of the minor complaints voiced by the farmer is the fox-hunter's omission to say " thank you " when gates are opened and held for his convenience. Seldom can haste be so

WITH THE PYTCHLEY

FRANK FREEMAN ABOUT TO THROW HOUNDS INTO THE GORSE. IT WILL BE NOTED THAT THE FIELD ARE HALTED AT A LITTLE DISTANCE SO AS TO AFFORD EVERY CHANCE TO GET A FOX AWAY.

imperative in the hunting field as to preclude these elementary courtesies, observance of which plays such an immense part in the relationship between the two parties.

Accidents.

In the great cosmopolitan crowds which form the hunting fields of to-day there must always be riders imperfectly instructed in matters of custom and procedure just as there are others who fall short of the higher standards of horsemanship. How could it be otherwise in this imperfect world? Thus accidents happen which should never happen and tempers are regrettably lost. A frequent cause of serious mishap (to put it at its worst) and, at the best, of recrimination and ill-feeling, is the practice of riding too close to a leader. Was it not Fred Archer who by way of justifying himself in the eyes of a Leicestershire field after an ugly contretemps, declared with some feeling, " Why I gave him a length and a half ! " The unvarying rule must be never to present one's horse at a fence in the wake of another until the leader is safely landed and away. Many bold horses decline to be baulked in the last stride and conscience-stricken effort to pull up short and avert disaster may be made all too late.

Kickers.

A common cause of accident, so commonplace indeed that apology seems due for referring to it, is the presence of so many kicking horses in the crowd and the inability of their riders to counteract the vice. No hunting season passes without the tale of legs, human or equine, broken through this agency while preventive measures seem almost ignored. Some horses kick through an exuberance of spirits born of too much corn and too little work, in which case the halving of one and the doubling of the other should effect a cure before November has run its course. Others, and the great majority, do so from nervousness, either inherent or acquired, through partnership with an irritating and uncongenial rider. A case occurs to mind of an old horse of impeccable habits.who was lent for a season during his owner's absence abroad. On his return he surprised and annoyed the latter by striking out viciously in every gateway—but a very few days elapsed before he dropped the bad habit as quickly as he had picked it up. With some people horses invariably seem to acquire the vice, but precisely what these riders do to set the animal's nerves on edge it would be hard to say. The main thing to prevent accidents is to keep the horse's mouth and attention occupied by means of the bridle, and his feet on the move. To stand anchored in a crowded gateway with hand outstretched the while one's horse clears a circle with his heels is to court unpopularity and abuse. In an endeavour to turn the tables on an accuser it is sometimes alleged in excuse that the offending horse had been touched or bumped into and that retaliation was thus justified. Let it be said at once that in the rough and tumble of the day a well-trained hunter can no more effect such delicacy than can a polo pony or a troop horse in the ranks. Vicious horses of course there are who can never be cured, and owners of such will do well to draft them without loss of time for the sake of their own peace of mind. Most insidious of all is the equine tendency to kick hounds, and sooner or later a horse thus addicted will surely land one in serious trouble. For weeks and months the animal may be safely manœuvred out of reach of the pack, but a day will come when a hound gallops into his heels, and then, before there is time to realise it, mischief is done. Anyone who has the misfortune to injure a hound will do best to acquaint one of the Hunt staff at once and an apology should be penned to the Master on arrival home. I know of a lady who signalised her first appearance with a famous pack many years ago by killing a hound stone dead. In the anguish and remorse which pursued her she found comfort in the kindly letter of sympathy which she received from the Master, one of the most charming gentlemen who ever carried a horn upon his saddle.

In a chapter such as this advice might be looked for as how best to enjoy hunting to the full, from the moment when the reins are first gathered up until horse and rider part at the close of the day. But what a difficult problem for the writer when one considers all the different points of view. Some people ride to hunt (as indeed they should), while others hunt to ride, and many more are well content without conspicuous concentration on either. The great exponents of the fine art of riding to hounds leave us their example and their coat-tails to follow as best we may. We marvel at their boldness, their quickness, and their consistency. How do they do it ? Galloping always between his fences and steadying his horse as he comes to the obstacle, the leader has ever an eye on the hounds, anticipating every turn and twist. Why should instinct infallibly lead one man to the best place in every fence just as surely as it leads another to the most impracticable spot ? Clearly the answer is that one possesses and the other lacks

that precious attribute which we term " an eye for a country."
Yet it is certain that all the arts and all the horses would fail
to carry a man day after day to the forefront of the field without the determination credited to the hero of Egerton
Warburton's hunting song :

> " . . . the man to whom naught comes amiss,
> One horse or another, that country or this,
> Through falls and bad starts who undauntedly still
> Lives up to the motto ' Be with them I will.' "

Enjoyment of hunting depends so much on the spirit in
which the game is played, and jealous riders or those given to
quarrel and recrimination will never get the best out of it.

Motors.

The advent of the motor car has exercised a greater influence
on the hunting field than any invention within the lifetime of
the present generation. It has changed many things in con-
nection with the sport and the change has been always for the
worse. We certainly claim that we can now get to the meet
in a quarter of the time that the journey formerly occupied,
and that we have leisure to attend to our correspondence and
so forth before we start. " When people say this," wrote the
late Lord Willoughby de Broke, " they generally mean that
the time can be comfortably devoted to lying in bed. But
granted that the busy man can leave the door at 10.15 a.m.
in a motor car instead of 9.30 a.m. in a carriage, is there much
real saving of tissue? The time between 9.30 a.m. and
10.15 a.m. might be more restfully spent in the phaeton or the
buggy than in talking on the telephone, interviewing the agent
or composing letters to creditors." How true it all is. However, for better or for worse the motor car is the covert hack
of to-day, and doubtless of to-morrow too, unless the aeroplane
comes to supersede it. What we have to do is to see that the
car is confined to its legitimate use and that it is not permitted
in any way to contravene the sportsman's code. Shocking
accusations against certain big game hunters who employ cars
have recently appeared in the Press, and it is up to all Masters
of Hounds, and to everyone who is jealous for the good name
of fox-hunting, to see that no mechanical aid is employed for
the purpose of killing a fox. The Masters of the Pytchley
Hounds have made it a practice to circularise all their followers,
asking them to send their cars straight home from the meet
and thus ensure that the drivers do not hang about and get in

the way. With motor horse-boxes increasing, as they are sure to do in the next few years, it will be even more necessary to issue orders for the removal of these cumbersome articles to some definite spot where they can be found when required.

The problem of the outside public and their cars is a much more delicate matter and it is seriously agitating the minds of the Masters of Hounds all over the country. The fact is, that there are quite a number of people to whom the possession of a motor car and the leisure to drive about in it are novelties of which they have scarcely learned to make the best use. They turn up at a meet of hounds not necessarily from any interest in hunting, and certainly with no desire to offend, but merely because they have nothing else to do. Other people will spend hours watching workmen dig up a London street, or the guests arriving at the wedding of people whose names they (the onlookers) do not even know, for no better reason. Quite unwittingly these motorists spoil sport day after day, more especially of course in the countries which are most inter-sected by roads. Rebuked by the Master for heading the fox they are genuinely hurt, having no idea that they were doing wrong. Indeed he requires some courage to address them at all for have they not precisely as much right to the King's high-way as is enjoyed by him and by those who hunt with his hounds ? Some form of propaganda may perhaps succeed in curbing their activities in due time, but meanwhile the nuisance grows and grows.

However, there is certainly no intention here to harp on the various little worries that beset the fox-hunter. Rather would I suggest that attention be concentrated on the brighter side of the picture. Through changing and difficult years (the Great War furnishes an eternal example) the flag of fox-hunting has remained nailed to the mast, and if the spirit remains the same in the future as it has been in the past, it will not easily be hauled down while the British flag remains flying. When difficulties beset, and we utter a sage pronouncement that " Times are not what they used to be," it is well to remember the wag's retort that " They never were."

Dress.

I do not suppose that fashion in the matter of dress and suchlike in the hunting field has seen, or is likely to see, any revolutionary change. The familiar sporting pictures of the nineteenth century, such as the CRICK MEET (which I merely mention since it hangs beside me now), show the fox-hunter

"HUNTING PIECE"

SIR ROBERT WALPOLE & HIS HOUNDS WITH COLONEL CHARLES CHURCHILL & MR. TURNER.
JOHN WOOTTON PINX.   SERPINIERE DEL.
PUBLISHED BY JOHN BOYELL.

attired very much as are we ourselves. Between Mr. Barraud's group and the gathering that would be depicted to-day there is of course the obvious and outstanding difference between a company of men and an assemblage where ladies are likely enough in the majority. Here is a sweeping change, you will agree, and assuredly it must be a change for the better. For many ladies life in a hunting country must have been decidedly boring for six months in the year ! What a difference too must their enrolment have made to the whole tone of the hunting field ! Feminine fashions which alter while those of the mere male stand still have of course undergone change since the hunter first carried a side-saddle, and there is of course all the difference in the world between the appearance of the flowing habits depicted by Leech and the apron skirt of to-day. The practice of riding astride is a recent innovation, and in most hunting fields nowadays there are ladies who in a cross saddle are capable of holding their own with the best when hounds run and who present a smart appearance too. With all deference to these exponents of the new method, however, the side-saddle remains and is likely to remain the safer, the smarter, and the better seat for the purpose with which we are concerned.

Until cub-hunting is at an end and the hunting season starts officially ladies and gentlemen are accustomed to regard themselves as free from all formalities in the matter of dress. Thus we see some curious turn-outs during September and October. Some Masters of Hounds may not care what people wear, but if the M.F.H. expresses any wishes in this matter they should be respected. I remember hearing the late Lord Annaly tell off a young gentleman for coming out cub-hunting in a cloth cap instead of a bowler hat. It would be well if other Masters took a similar line to-day for there is nothing so infectious as slackness. We see caps, jerseys such as racing stable lads affect, jodhpur breeches, and heaven knows what besides. As for the musical comedy effects which some of the fair sex manage to achieve, one feels bound to write, if it may be set down without offence, that these are out of keeping with the practical atmosphere of the hunting field. I have heard of a Master ante-dating his opening day by a week for the reason that, he averred, he could bear the sight of these things no longer. When November comes all is plain sailing. Then at all events we know where we are. In the matter of the scarlet coat the present-day fox-hunter has well maintained the conservatism of former generations. From every point of view it is well that this should be so. There is nothing else so warm, so serviceable, and so smart. Why a black coat or habit made of good stout " Melton " cloth should not turn the rain like a red one, is a question I cannot answer. I can only relate my experience. Perhaps there is some magic property in the dye that makes the latter more waterproof. I could, if personal reminiscence is permissible, quote an instance of two coats purchased in time for the hunting season of 1919-21 which did duty jointly four days in every normal week for three consecutive seasons, and I am prepared to state that during that time neither of them was ever really wet through. That Monday in November on which the first of these garments was donned was a memorable day not merely in the life of the wearer, but in that of England herself, for the " old red rag," save as worn by the Hunt servants, had not been seen in the land since the spring of 1914. There had been days in that unforgettable interval when those least given to pessimism must have felt a secret doubt as to the future of the fine old sport which was always in their hearts and their thoughts. A red coat, to hark back to our subject, has something else to recommend it besides warmth and durability. In an age with conspicuously small regard for old institutions and customs, its colour still commands a measure of respect in the country-side. When we put it on we desire to pay some compliment to those over whose land we are going to ride, and I believe that the feeling is appreciated. It may be said that if damage is done or annoyance caused, the personality of the transgressor does not make things any better or worse; be he the finished product of Melton or garbed *per contra* like the conventional rat-catcher, a broken rail is a broken rail. In point of fact, the average farmer draws a very real distinction in such matters, and if a day should come when the fox-hunter ceases to pay due regard to outward appearances and convention his welcome will not be the same as it has been in the past or as it is to-day.

In the matter of present fashions there is no outstanding change that I am aware of to record. Hat crowns are a little lower perhaps, coat tails a little shorter. It was said that Beau Brummel's orders to his tailor were to " keep continually sending leather breeches," but for the moment these seem to be out of favour, which is a thousand pities. For comfort and smartness there is nothing to equal them and to set against a higher initial cost is the practical certainty that you will never wear them out. When Lord Lonsdale had the Quorn

Hounds his men were all turned out in leather breeches, and he relates that Tom Firr, after wearing them, was wont to declare that he had never known what it was to ride in real comfort before. The Belvoir servants likewise wore leathers during the Mastership of Lord Daresbury (then Sir Gilbert Greenall), and I believe that he considered them a positive economy. The fashionable colour for boot-tops, a very light shade of brown, is almost identical with what our forbears affected half a century ago, but as at all times latitude is permitted for individual tastes. Many people now wear boots with polished tops similar to those worn by Hunt servants. Provided they are not allowed to become stained or scarred, these present, as we all know, a thoroughly workmanlike appearance, and the ease with which they can be cleaned is a recommendation in this practical age. Hunting whips have become shorter nowadays and are frequently much too short for the purpose they are intended for, that of opening gates. Spurs are likewise shorter than heretofore, but here the change appears decidedly for the better. In matters of dress and equipment it will probably pay the fox-hunter to choose the clothes, etc., that suit him, and stick to these without regard to the fashions of the moment. A great-uncle of the present writer (a friend and contemporary of the late Mr. Tailby) always had his hunting hats made to the same pattern, and used to declare that though there were years when his headgear appeared out of date, there were other times when he was surprised to find himself in the height of fashion.

The best of London tailors, bootmakers, and saddlers seem to possess the art of turning out goods that never wear out, and to deal with such tradesmen is therefore the height of economy. All that we need to do is to see that their products are duly cared for. Second-rate equipment is dear at any price. The best of everything should be good enough, and only just good enough for the fox-hunter.

The Etiquette

I HAVE written a fair amount in this book on what is really "etiquette," and in consequence I thought it unnecessary to devote a separate chapter to it, yet the subject is so important that I will tell you all I can think of on the subject, and if some of it does not seem to you to be entirely etiquette you must understand that I have mentioned this particular matter because it refers to your general deportment in the field, and that, probably, in direct reference as to how you can help in the hunt.

I suppose the first thing I must tell you to do is to raise your hat to the Master and wish him "good-morning" on your arrival at the meet. Talking of "good-mornings," it may seem curious to you that in hunting language there is never any "good-afternoon." No matter how early in the afternoon it may be that you leave the hunt, or you may be speeding from the hunt some parting guest; it is always "good-night." That to you may seem funny. It will sound funnier to you, I can assure you, just after lunchtime! Do not force your company upon any of the "high ones "—the Master, the Field Master, if the Master hunts his own hounds, the secretary, and prominent landowners, and so on. You should, however, make a point of saying "good-morning" to the huntsman, whom you should address by his surname, and the whippers-in, whom you should call by their Christian names. That's funny, too, in a way.

And while on the subject of greetings and talkings, you should, as a young entry, be as unobtrusive as you can. Even if you have companions of the same age and experience, do avoid talking when hounds are drawing. Talk as much as you like when moving between the coverts, but not otherwise. If you *have* to talk about anything, do so in a very low voice. Do not talk to either of the whippers-in; they are on duty, and the watching of a covert requires a great deal of real concentration.

I have noticed that certain people like to talk about their own performances, and by this I don't necessarily mean in a boasting way, and to tell you how their horses jumped this and that. Avoid giving the idea that you and your horse are exceptional performers. If you did talk about it, most likely it would be because of your natural enthusiasm after a good hunt, but, anyway, that sort of thing is not looked upon with favour.

When in a lane and hounds are passing you,

always turn your horse's head to hounds with his back to the hedge. This turning of the head applies when meeting any one hound or more. If heels must kick it should be into the air, not into hounds. Always pull into your near side if the huntsman or whipper-in comes galloping behind you in a lane or "ride." If the huntsman appears from nowhere—a tiresome habit which they seem to acquire in woodland countries—make way at once, just as fast as ever you can, and to those in front of you yell out "Huntsman" as loud as ever you can. If the huntsman is riding to an obstacle which you believe must be man-handled, something pulled down or opened or removed, race behind him to it and give a hand, and if the first whipper-in is there first, hold his horse or push or pull with him.

Hunting whips are useless things, for about the only time you will need yours will be for opening gates and holding them open. Actually with a handy horse it is much easier to do this with the fingers, especially as practically no gate works smoothly, nor does any latch or chain. The thong and lash are particularly useless except perhaps to haul on to when opening a gate and your horse steps back. A hunting whip is a bad thing to hit a horse with as it is too heavy, and as you must never strike a hound with your whip it is hard to see why we carry them; an expanding hook would

IF THE HUNTSMAN APPEARS FROM NOWHERE.

be much more useful at the gate and a cutting whip more useful on the horse! However, there it is. You will be carrying your whip, anyway, but don't crack it; you may hit yourself, your horse, your neighbour, or all three, and cause a lot of unpleasantness. It's very nice if you *can* crack a whip well, but it's better done in the garden, and you may get a chance hunting if you have to do a rodeo after intruding cattle and horses.

It is against etiquette to meet the hunt at the first draw: you should always go to the meet and be there before the appointed time. When you are moving down a road and a car is coming up behind the riders, be sure not only to make way for it, but to call to others to do likewise. Everyone, remember, is entitled to the use of the road, and the slower must give place to the faster.

Wherever you find something when you are galloping which may cause trouble, such as rabbit holes, hidden "grips" or small ditches, harrow overgrown with grass—anything, in fact, likely to bring a horse down—throw your voice over your shoulder to the man behind you and yell out, "'Ware so and so" (pronounced "war"). It is usually sufficient to say, "'Ware hole," and the fact that you haven't described the terror is of no particular moment. It's the yell that does it. Many a fall has been saved in this way, and it is

. . . FOR OPENING GATES AND HOLDING THEM OPEN . . . .

very much a case with you of, "Do as you would be done by."

Always give way at a jump to anyone in charge of a young boy or girl; by this I mean you must do your best not to separate them. Although I am all in favour of sticking to your rights, the chief one of which is that you take your turn if necessary, and class and age do not come into it, yet I would plead also for the person who is obviously in difficulties with a young or troublesome horse. If your horse refuses, you must on no account turn him and have another cut at the jump, but must pull round and join the queue, as it were.

Here is no question of etiquette, but humanity or good sportsmanship, or call it what you will, demands that you should stand by the fallen, and don't leave them until you are satisfied that you have done what you can.

Nothing is more discourteous than for anyone to ride through a gate and let it swing to after him without holding it for the man who is coming behind. You should always look back to see if anyone is following, and although no one can expect you to hold a gate for any time longer than a few seconds, again you must do as you would be done by, and if you do leave the gate try to let it go in such a way that it is easily opened by the man who follows.

And talking of gates—always set out for your day's hunting with a few sixpences in your pocket. There will be various farm hands, village boys and girls standing to hold gates open for you, all out to see a bit of the fun. It is, to my mind, speaking of these abominable gates which never open well, worth while to have them opened at sixpence a time! There is another and very good reason for distributing a little silver, and that is that it fosters goodwill in the countryside by adding a little pleasure to the villager's day with his own pack of hounds.

Be very careful when hounds are running not to override them in any circumstances. More than this, do not crowd them, and certainly, again in no circumstances, cut off any hound from the pack. You will realize that it is very distracting to hounds to have the field galloping close on their heels, and it is almost sure to make them lift their heads if anyone should come too close. I know it is a great temptation in a big open country, especially on downland when hounds get away on a good scent, to race along almost parallel with the tail hounds. It is, I can assure you, a very unwise thing to do, for at any moment the pack may stop or swerve violently, and you'll be among them in a moment and in trouble with the huntsman.

Always do your best to catch a loose horse and always return it to the unfortunate owner, who has presumably taken a toss. Having returned it, be sure to see that he is mounted and give him a hand in mounting if necessary. Very likely he is a bit shaken, or perhaps worse than that. If he talks "stoopid," as they say in the country, he's concussed, so stand by him and don't leave him. Conduct him tactfully to the road and hand him over to someone if you can. These cases are rather difficult sometimes and the patient usually very pig-headed.

Just because you are riding a kicker with a little red bow on his tail, don't think you can ride unconcerned in the crowd at gates or in narrow rides. You must always ride such a horse with due consideration for others, having regard to his vice.

Finally, let me say that any stranger to your hunt is a guest of the hunt, even if he has to pay for the privilege of hunting, and you must be sure to extend to him the welcome which you would wish to receive yourself.

All breaches of etiquette are forgiven and forgotten, but if unhappily your horse should kick a hound, forgiveness is long delayed and the episode never forgotten!

The Language

MANY people think that there is a lot of etiquette in the hunting-field and that the novice has to go through a rather trying period learning a number of customs and things to do and things not to do. From the point of view of the novice who has this prospect before him it all sounds rather alarming, and it is certainly not likely to be made any easier by reason of the fact that the novice has never or hardly ever ridden to hounds, and a horse out for a quiet hack is very often an angel compared to the same devil out hunting. Naturally enough the beginner is anxious that he and his horse should not disgrace themselves, but what with this and what with that the prospect does look a little formidable.

Well, my advice to the novice is not to take too much notice of all this hunting custom, hunting etiquette, and so on. It's all simple enough and founded on common sense, and there is no need to think just because you are a beginner and may get in the way of someone that you are going to have your head bitten off. The hunting-field is not peopled by blue-faced colonels of the H. M. Bateman type who are as near to bursting as makes no matter. Anyway, if you should come across one and what you did was not your fault or was within your right or was nobody's fault—well, let him burst. Remember all are equal in the hunting-field and the prior right of way goes only to the huntsman, the whippers-in, and the Master. With all others it is take your turn, kickers to the rear.

There is one subject, however, which you should know, and that is the language, and although you will pick most of it up in course of time it will be as well for me to talk to you a little about it. First of all there is no need to alter your language when you are hunting to the extent of calling it "huntin'"; nor to talk of "'ems" and "'uns," in spite of some novelists, who appear to think that such enunciation is inseparable from hunting people.

I suppose the very first word we must mention is *hounds*. I need not tell you that a hound should never be called a "dog"; if you slipped to that extent it would be too awful, and yet funnily enough, or so it may seem, you must always refer to the *dog-pack* as distinct from the *bitch-pack*, never hound-pack. Again, supposing you and I are standing at the meet looking at hounds and the pack is a mixed one, I should say to you, for example, "Look at that heavily marked *dog* over there," to distinguish him, you see, from a bitch. You must never refer to two hounds or three hounds, but always to a *couple of hounds* or *one and a half couple*, as the case may be, and *three and a half couple* and so on. *A brace of foxes*, remember, not two foxes, and the rest of it as before: "*We killed one and a half brace.*"

Now something about fences and other jumps. You will have heard of a *bull-finch*; this is a hedge so high that you cannot jump it, but not so thick that you cannot jump partly over and partly through. Posts and rails are sometimes called such, but generally speaking *timber*; and an *oxer* is a fence (hedge) with a rail on one side to protect it from cattle breaking it down. If there is a similar rail on the other side, as very likely there will be, this is called a *double oxer*, and I can assure you that it makes a very formidable obstacle. A *cut and laid* is a nice jump to take if it is reasonably low, because it is easy to see as a rule. It consists of a hedge cut hard back, the top is cut off, or some of it nearly off, and laced or twined sideways along the top of the hedge. A *stake and bound* consists of upright stakes bound horizontally. I need not say that a jump with a *ditch on the near side* means you have first a ditch and then the hedge. A hedge, by the way, is always called a *fence*. I have called it hedge to make my meaning clear, for to the novice a fence may mean a wooden fence.

You will often see the word *holloa* in print. This is pronounced *holler*, and means what it says—someone has let one go indicating that he has seen a fox; and, by the way, *huick holloa* is *hike holler*, which means listen, or "Hark, there is a holler." Hounds never bark, by the way, but *speak* to a line or scent. This is properly called *owning the line*; a curious phrase, I always think, but rather expressive.

If a hound has a *good nose*, it does not mean that physically that portion of him is something to admire, it merely means that he has good scenting powers, that he can pick up a scent well. And if a nose is not really a nose, certainly a tail is never a tail, it is always a *stern*. A dog may wag his tail but a hound waves his stern. Hounds will often lose the scent of a fox when the latter crosses some land which has recently had, say, artificial manure put on it, or on which sheep have been penned and which in some ways has acquired a strong unnatural smell, or even temporarily by cattle or sheep having just gone across it. Such land is called *foiled* and delights the heart of a hunted fox.

To *cap* anyone following hounds on a horse is the job of the secretary or his deputy, and means that the persons concerned, and it only concerns those who do not subscribe, is asked to pay for his day's enjoyment. The amount depends largely on the particular hunt, and in some of the more fashionable this cap may amount to as much as three guineas a day, and is imposed to keep down the numbers who hunt with them.

Very often just before a hound, or, as far as that goes, several hounds, own the line—that is, get on to the scent of a fox—you will see them taking a sudden and much more active interest; they move more quickly, their noses seem more glued to the ground, and their sterns move furiously from side to side. This is called *feathering*. After this you may expect the pack to sweep away on the line and to *give tongue*, which is called the *cry* of hounds or *music*. Don't for goodness' sake ever say "bark."

Now here's a funny thing. You can understand that covering a large expanse of country during the course of a hunt the pack will meet a number of animals of all sorts, including perhaps a dog or two. No matter of what shape, size, or breed, any such is called a *cur-dog*, which seems most impolite and suggests that a foxhound—for he alone is *not* a cur-dog—is something very superior. There is something rather arrogant about this, I think. Well, I suppose on hunting days hounds are entitled to look upon themselves as removed from the common kennel.

A phrase which is not entirely descriptive but which must not be forgotten is *breaking up* a fox. On the face of it the idea presents difficulties, almost insuperable. Actually when hounds kill their fox and individuals are enjoying such portions as they may have seized and others are having fights over other remnants which they would enjoy, they are *breaking up their fox*.

You would never talk of a wood being very muddy to describe how you ploughed down a *ride*, which is a path or roadway in such wood, in which your horse sinks up to his knees or hocks in mud. Such a wood is described as *riding very deep*. If these rides are very overgrown they need *brushing*. To "brush" the rides means that the bushes and trees on either side are well cut back.

A *bag-fox*—well, perhaps you can guess what he is? Sometimes in order to ensure a hunt or to give a fox a chance, one that has been secured in some way, perhaps dug out of an earth, has been carried in a bag to the desired spot and released. This, I may say, is "not done" in the ordinary way, but is resorted to sometimes where some part of the country has too many foxes and another too few.

As I have said elsewhere, cub-hunting begins at such time of the year as circumstances suggest. Hunting proper begins on the first of November or the nearest day of the week after that on which the particular pack hunts. In other words, the hunt does not of necessity meet on November 1st. Sometimes a hunt is arranged and does not appear in the regular *hunt appointment card*, which usually takes the form of a list of forthcoming meets sent to subscribers on a postcard. This is called a *bye-day*.

During early cub-hunting the hedges are naturally in full summer leaf, the ditches are all overgrown, and it is very difficult to see far ahead and dangerous to jump. This state of affairs exists in varying degrees right up to the opening meet, and, if the frosts have been delayed or are very slight, until later. The country under these conditions is said to ride very *blind*, a good and descriptive word, I think.

Perhaps I have now given you an idea of the more usual words and phrases which you will hear spoken in the hunting-field or when people are discussing hunting. Those which you will not find in this chapter you will find probably elsewhere in this book, or else I have omitted reference to them because they are words which you are unlikely to come across, though strictly in the hunting language; or again, some may be words which seem hardly necessary to mention as they are obvious slang. Among these would be a *thruster*, who, as the name implies, may be found in front of the hunt, a reckless fellow who will be among the first when the pack pull down their fox and probably a brave fellow, too. Another such word might be a *voluntary*—" to *cut a voluntary*," which is not strictly a hunting term, but which, as we all know, means a fall.

There is, however, one word, or rather three words, which I have kept to the last, and it is a case of which word shall we use: *Scarlet? Red? Pink?* I always say that scarlet is the word, and that no other must be used; this is correct, I think, because it is, so far as one can trace, the original term. It does not seem to matter so much except, as I have written before, it is as well to be as accurate as possible. It is certain that whatever word you use you will be understood.

Probably before the end of your first season you will hear all these words and expressions used. Probably you will use a number of them yourself. My advice, however, to you is: for the first season or two keep your eyes open and your mouth shut, and at every jump *throw your heart over first.* This apparently rather difficult feat is, I am quite certain, the thing which saves numberless falls. That seems absurd, but the amount of confidence which it gives to a horse is incalculable.

WHAT IS THAT?

WHAT IS THAT?

A

"All On!"—A pack is "All on" when every hound comprising it is present. Upon leaving a covert, and at the end of the day's sport, a whipper-in counts ("makes") the pack, and, if all are present, reports "All On, sir!" If some are missing, he reports "Want a couple and a half, sir!" or whatever the number may be.

Apron.—A water-proof apron worn by a fox-hunter to keep the lower limbs dry without the necessity of clumbering himself with a mackintosh.

A wooden inverted V placed, by a hunt, over a wire-fence in order to make it safe to jump. See *Hen-coop.*

Artificial Earth.—A refuge for foxes, made by a hunt, with the object of encouraging foxes to breed or lie in a certain part of its country; it usually consists of two lengths of drain-pipe and a small chamber, as bedroom, where they meet; but there are many forms, some extremely simple, others fitted with all modern conveniences, from h. *&* c. to air conditioning.

B

Babble.—A hound is said to babble, or to be a "babbler," when it throws its tongue unnecessarily: *e.g.* when it is far behind the leading hounds, or, in covert, without the line of a fox.

Back at the knee.—To be back at the knee is a fault in conformation of both hounds and horses. When viewed from the side, the knee and fore-arm appear to be behind the vertical level of the lower leg.

Back, to.—To "back a horse" is to ride it for the first time in its life.

Back-raking.—Back-raking is the process of inserting the hand and arm into a horse's anus to remove any impediment which may be causing a stoppage.

Bag-fox.—A bag-fox, bagged-fox, or "bagman," is a fox which is turned out of a sack, enclosure, or drain into which it has previously been put, in order that it may be hunted.

Ball.—A ball is an equine or canine pill. To "ball" is to administer a pill; a ball-gun is an instrument used for the administration of a pill to a horse (designed to prevent the baller's hand being removed and swallowed instead of the ball); balling is the process of administering a ball.

Bars.—A horse has two sets of bars: there are the bars of his mouth—the portion of un-toothed gums upon which a curb-bit acts and there are the bars of the foot, about which more may be learnt by studying the diagram of a foot.

Bedding.—The litter upon which horses or hounds lie when resting.

Bed-down.—To bed-down is to put down a horse's bed.

Belvoir tan.—A foxhound colour, in other days extremely *comme il faut*. It is a very dark rich tan or mahogany, with black markings on the body, but no white (save possibly a white collar) above the elbows.

Benches.—The wooden platforms upon which hounds sleep in kennels are known as "benches."

Billett.—A billett is a fox's excreta or droppings.

Binder.—The horizontal top thin branch of a cut-and-laid fence.

Bit.—As everybody knows, a bit is a steel, or part-steel instrument placed in a horse's mouth with the hope that man may thereby be enabled to control the horse—frequently it remains a hope. What everybody does not realise is that "bit" when used in conjunction with the words "—and bridoon," or in the assumed conjunction with those words, means a curb-bit (*q.v.*)

Blank.—A covert is blank when it does not hold a fox. A blank day is a day on which no fox is found.

Blind.—A fence is "blind" when the exact edge of the ditch facing it, or the exact outline of the bank comprising it, is hidden by grass, etc. A country is said to be "blind" when there is still much leaf and old grass about the fences.

Blood.—To blood hounds is to kill a fox with them and let them break it up. To blood young hounds is to give them their first kill. To blood a child, or a fox-hunting novitiate, is to smear his, her, or its cheeks with the blood of a recently killed fox. If he, she, or it, is to grow into a real fox-hunter this blood must never be washed off, but must be allowed to wear off. It is customary to present the hunt servant with a *pour boire* when a grown-up novitiate is blooded.

A pack which is said to be "out of blood" has not killed a fox for a long time, while one which is "in blood" has recently killed several foxes in close succession.

Blowing away.—A huntsman blows his hounds away from a covert, with quick, pulsating, notes of the horn, on to the line of a fox; "blowing away" is therefore the prelude to a hunt in the open.

Blowing out.—A huntsman blows his hounds out of a blank covert with long mournful wails of the horn.

Bob-tailed.—A bob-tailed fox is one without a brush, or with a very short brush, "the result of an accident."

Body-brush.—A grooming-brush, oval-shaped and made of stout short bristles, with which the bulk of the grooming of a horse should be done.

Boiler.—The large open vat in which the pudding or flesh for hounds is boiled . . . Also, the kennelman who acts as chef to the kennels.

Bolt.—Of horses, to run away out of the rider's control or, if followed by "his food," to gobble his meals in the manner of a small and disgusting child (a process which is frequently accompanied by its own reward, indigestion).

Of foxes, to force them out of a drain or an earth with the aid of a terrier, drain-brush, stick, or any other adversity.

Bone.—The size and strength of a horse or a hound is usually measured by its "bone": that is, by the circumference of its leg immediately beneath the knee; an animal with "plenty of bone" is strong.

Bots.—The larvæ of the gadfly, looking like small white specks on the ends of the hairs. They pass by means of the tongue into the stomach, where they may cause debility.

Bottom.—No, madam, *not* that. To a fox-hunter, a bottom means only one thing—a big deep ditch. In some parts of England, a bottom is simply a very large ditch accompanied by a very large fence, the whole being the lowest part of its own small valley and, in all probability, the boundary fence of its own farm. In other, less fashionable, parts a bottom is first cousin to a ravine or chasm, and probably contains a small river, trees, a bog, and a wire fence. It may also be called, in that case, a Dingle, a Ghyll, a Gill, a Dene, a Coombe. a Combe, or, by fox-hunters, a———

Box, loose.—A partitioned-off area in a stable in which a horse lives, confined by the partitions, but loose.

Box, to.—To box a hunter is to send it to the meet, or the point-to-point or other engagement by train, by motor horse-box, or by motor horse-trailer.

Break.—A fox "breaks", or "breaks covert", when he leaves a covert or woodland for the open.

Break up.—A kennelman breaks up oatmeal pudding before it is fed to the pack. This he does after transferring it from the "cooler" to the "trough"; at the same time he mixes it with broth (that is, the liquid result of boiled horse or cow), or, if he is foolish and ignorant, with water.

A pack breaks up a fox when they "Who-oop! Tear 'im and eat 'im!"

Break out.—A horse breaks out when he sweats, frequently from nervous causes, after being groomed, usually at the end of a day's hunting or racing.

Breast-plate.—Is an article of equine apparel, designed to fit neatly round the shoulders and to prevent the saddle slipping backwards when going up steep places. It is always unsightly and usually unnecessary.

Broken knees.—Are not as alarming as they sound. The break here refers to the skin and not of necessity to the bone. Broken knees are a blemish.

Brow band.—Another article of equine apparel. It fits round the front and top of the face, just below and in front of the ears. It should always be made of plain, brown, leather when worn by hunters and civilian riding horses—never should it be coloured. A coloured brow-band is to the hunter what a made-up tie is to its owner; frequently, coloured brow-bands and made-up ties are found in the same establishment.

Brush.—A fox's brush is his tail.

A horse is said to brush when he knocks the fetlock joint of one leg against the fetlock joint of the other leg.

Brushing-boots.—These are worn by horses, not to prevent brushing, but to prevent sore fetlock joints, which are the effects of brushing.

Bullfinch.—A thorn fence, too high to be jumped over, and frequently too thick to be jumped through.

Butcher.—A Master of Fox-hounds or a huntsman is said to be a butcher when he kills more foxes than the person using the expression thinks he should kill.

A horseman is said to be a butcher when he rides a horse very badly, or rides it too hard.

Butcher-boots.—These are plain, long, black, boots without tops, worn with "rat-catcher" or with a silk hat, black coat, and coloured breeches.

Button, Hunt.—Every hunt has its own button, consisting of a black (worn on a black coat) or a brass (worn on a red coat) button engraved with the monogram or initials of the hunt, or some other design. It should only be worn by a subscriber to or official of that hunt, at the invitation of the Master; in some hunts this invitation is understood by all persons subscribing a certain sum to the coffers of the Hunt, in others the button is only worn upon the expressed desire of the Master.

Bye-day.—An extra hunting-day; an unadvertised hunting-day; a hunting-day above the normal quota of the week (*i.e.* a two-day-a-week pack may hunt three days in one week: the third day is a bye-day). Ordinary fox-hunting dress should be worn on a bye-day; but on such a day the Master is at liberty to do what he likes, even to go home without trying to find a fox if he feels so inclined; accordingly, few hunts take a cap from strangers on a bye-day.

C

Calkin.—A calkin is a protrusion from the heel of a horse's shoe, designed to afford him a better grip. They are suitable only for draught horses, not for riding horses.

Cap.—The controversial head-gear worn by M.F.H., Hunt Staff, Field-Master, Secretary, visiting-and ex-M.F.H., farmers, their several wives, and—apparently—anybody else who knows no better. It is covered with black velvet.

A sum of money extracted by the secretary of a hunt from those persons, not being subscribers, visiting the hunt for the day; this sum, varying from 10*s.* to £3, goes to Hunt Funds.

A sum of money, extracted by the Secretary or a person or persons appointed by him, from all those hunting, less the Hunt Staff. This sum, usually 2*s*. 6*d*., goes to the Wire or Poultry Fund.

Capped.—A horse's elbow or hock is said to be capped when it is covered by a large, fluid bag, or enlargement. These enlargements are blemishes, not causes of unsoundness.

Carry.—Ploughland is said to carry when, after a frost, it is sticky and adheres to feet of fox and hounds.

Carry a scent.—Good scenting land "carries a scent."

Carry the scent.—Those hounds of a pack carry the scent which, at a given moment, are actually smelling the fox's scent.

Cast.—An effort on the part of the pack to recover the fox's line after a check; the pack may make a cast on their own account or at the bidding of their huntsman.

Cat-foot.—The normal, round, ball or catlike foot of the fox-hound. Some hounds, in particular fell-hounds, have hare feet, which are longer.

Catch hold.—Of a horse: to pull.

Of a huntsman: to catch hold of the pack is to lift the pack (*q.v.*).

Chaff.—Chopped hay or straw, or hay and straw, used as food for horses and as bedding for puppies and pigs.

Challenge.—A hound which endorses the opinion of the first hound to open on a fox is said to "challenge." Challenge may also, less correctly, be used for "open."

Check.—Hounds check when they are unable any longer to follow the scent trail of the fox. A check is the period of time during which the hounds are checked.

Chop.—A fox is said to be "chopped" when he is killed while still asleep or before he has run more than a few yards.

Clean.—A horse or hound is said to be "nice and clean" when there is no "neck-cloth" and no coarseness about the line of the neck.

Ground is said to be "clean" when it is not foiled or stained (*q.v.*).

Close a cast.—To close the cast is to make good all the ground in a complete circle round the spot at which hounds checked.

Cogs, frost.—Frost cogs are small protuberances made to be screwed into previously prepared sockets in a horse's shoes. Their business end is sharpened, and their function is to give the horse a firmer foothold on ice-bound roads. They are not the same as frost-nails, which see.

Cold-back.—A horse is said to have a cold back when he not only flinches when the saddle is put on his back but also bucks, lies down, runs away or otherwise disports if the saddle is occupied shortly after saddling: to over-come the difficulty his back is given, say, twenty minutes, to "warm" after saddling.

Colic.—Equine tummy-ache, produced by a variety of causes and of a variety of degrees of venom and danger.

Collect.—To collect a horse is to "ride him 'twixt hand and heel." According to the *Manual of Equitation and Horsemastership*, "a horse is said to be collected when his head is raised and bent at the poll, the jaw relaxed, and the hocks brought well under him, so that he has the maximum control over his limbs and is in a position to respond instantly to the least indication of his rider." So now you know.

Concave shoes.—These shoes are so shaped that the ground surface is narrower than the bearing surface. Most hunter shoes, for the sake of lightness, are concave.

Condition.—"A horse is said to be in condition when he is physically fit to undertake without strain the ordinary work which he may be required to perform. Such condition can only be secured by a gradual process of preparation and attention to detail." So says the *Manual of Equitation and Horsemastership*. "Condition" means one thing for a race-horse, another for a hunter; one thing for the huntsman's horse, another for the horse of the Father of the Hunt, *aetat* 107.

Cooked.—Such is the cruelty of fox-hunters that they cook their horses alive. A cooked horse is one that is dead beat after a hard gallop, probably owing to lack of condition. After death, a cooked horse is spoken of as "boiled," when fed to hounds, and as "beef" when fed to humans.

Cooler.—The cooler is a tray into which the hot oatmeal porridge is transferred, after cooking, from the copper; it has, generally, a zinc bottom and low wooden sides, perhaps 6 inches high. In this cooler the pudding sets into a flat-ish, solid, mass.

Copper.—The kennel boilers, in which the pudding and flesh are boiled, are spoken of as "coppers."

Country.—The area in which a hunt may draw for a fox is said to be its "country"; it may run a fox outside its country, and may even kill one outside, provided it does so without the use of terrier or without "breaking ground."

Couple.—Two foxhounds. The size of a pack is spoken of in terms of couples—*e.g.* 22½ couple. But one hound, all by itself is not "a half-couple"—or should not be—but is "one hound"; it only becomes a half couple when coupled with at least one other couple.

Couples.—Two leather hound-collars attached by links or a chain of steel, and used to join two hounds together so that neither can escape; couples are carried on Hunt Servant's saddles at all times.

Course.—Hounds are said to course a fox when they run it in view.

Court.—The paved, flagged, or concreted court-yard attached to each lodging room at kennels is called a "court."

Covert.—To a fox-hunter, all woods are "coverts," unless they happen to be woodlands. (*q.v.*)

Cracked heel.—A horse is said to suffer from a cracked heel when a heel is sore and greasy, or sore or greasy; cracked heels, also known as greasy heels, are usually due to neglect on the part of the horse-keeper, in failing to dry the heels when wet; at times they are due to constitutional causes.

Crib-biting.—A horse crib-bites when he catches a manger, wall, or other protruding object, with his teeth, arches his neck, and then swallows air. It is a stable-vice.

Crooked.—A foxhound is said to be crooked when his fore-legs are not straight when viewed from in front.

Cross-bred.—A hound which contains some Welsh, as well as English, blood, is sometimes spoken of as being "cross bred" or "Curre bred," or "Curre type." or "a bloody Welshman."

Cry.—The music of the pack is its cry. To be in full cry merely means that the majority of the pack are speaking to their fox.

Cub.—A young fox; after the Opening Meet there are no cubs.

Cur-dog.—In the hunting-field, and at all times to a Hunt Servant, any dog other than a foxhound is a cur-dog, no matter how blue blooded it may be in its own inferior breed.

Curb.—A curb is a bony enlargement protruding from the back of a horse's hock; it is a source of lameness, and so a technical unsoundness.

Curb-bit.—A curb-bit is a curb-bit.

Curb-chain.—A curb-chain is a chain used with a curb-bit.

Curly stern.—A foxhound is said to have a curly stern or a "gay" stern when his stern, or tail, has a kink in it.

Curre.—Sir Edward Curre was a breeder and Master of a very well-known pack of cross-bred hounds; these cross-bred hounds are now sometimes called "Curre" hounds, even though they may have no blood from his pack in them. See *Cross-bred* above.

Curry-comb.—A grooming tool, upon which the body-brush should be wiped occasionally in order to rid it of accumulated dirt; it should not be used on clipped horses.

Cutting.—Is an injury to the inside of a horse's coronet, where the horn and hoof join, caused by the horse striking the one leg with the inside of the opposite shoe, or by the clenches on the inside of the opposite foot.

Cut-and-laid.—A fence, of which the thorns comprising it are half-cut through and bent over.

D

Dandy-brush.—A grooming brush, made of fairly long, yellow, bristles set in a wooden back. The object of the dandy-brush is to remove surface mud and dirt from the horse before he is groomed with the body-brush; they are also used for brushing manes and tails; staple food of foxhound puppies.

Ditch, from you; to you.—A ditch from you is a ditch on the landing side of a fence. A ditch to you is a ditch on the take-off side of a fence.

Dock, the.—The dock of a horse is the bony part of its tail. A docked horse is a horse which has had its tail shortened so that only a part of the bone remains.

Doped foxes.—A doped fox is a fox which has had its natural scent augmented by artificial means at human instigation: in other words, a fox which has been "touched up" by aniseed or other canine-loved smell. A bad huntsman, who can earn a reputation for giving good sport in no other way, at times sinks to the depth of "doping his foxes." The most fashionable method is to introduce a fox (purchased for about £1 from a poacher in the neighbouring hunt's country) into a drain overnight, stopping it in; it is then bolted, and in the process is either sprinkled with the "dope" by a slick whipper-in innocently leaning over the mouth of the drain, or it paddles through a previously prepared puddle of dope at the mouth of the drain. Most hounds decline to break up "doped" foxes.

Double, a.—A double is a fence with a ditch on both sides.

Double-bank.—A double-bank is a bank, probably wide, with a ditch on both sides.

Double-bridle.—A double-bridle is a bridle which supports two bits in the horse's mouth—usually a bit-and-bridoon, or curb-and-snaffle.

Double-oxer.—A double-oxer is a thorn fence with an ox-rail on both sides. (See Oxer.)

Double-whiskey.—A double-whiskey is, as all the world knows, the staple diet and only nourishment of fox-hunters.

Double the horn.—A huntsman "doubles his horn" when he blows quick pulsating notes on it; *e.g.*, when a fox crosses a ride or is holloaed away. The horn is only doubled when a fox is a-foot.

Draft.—To draft a hound is to separate it from the pack. "The draft" is therefore a collection of hounds which, because they are no good to him, the Master separates from his pack with a view to their being sold or shot. To buy a draft is to buy such a collection of hounds. An unentered draft consists of unentered puppies; an entered draft of entered hounds—drafted, presumably, because of some fault. The day before hunting, the huntsman drafts the hunting-pack away from the rest of the hounds, into a separate kennel.

Drag.—The line of a fox leading to his kennel; to hunt *the* drag is to hunt this line up to the sleeping fox. This method of finding foxes is often used on moorland (*c.f.* drawing for a fox in covert, where the sleeping fox is actually winded by a hound).

A drag is also an artificial scenting line, made by dragging an evil-smelling rag along the ground. To hunt *a* drag is to hunt such a line. The fox-hunter should beware of using "a" when he means "the"— the mistake may mean a black-eye, or, in the barely civilised countries in which *the* drag is still hunted, a good old-fashioned horse-whipping.

Drain.—An underground drain-pipe used as a sleeping-place or refuge by foxes.

A large ditch, without fence.

A small ditch draining moorland, into which a galloping horse invariably puts one foot, so breaking its rider's neck.

To be a "rare horse over a drain" may mean that he will jump his "twice twelve foot of water" with ease, or that he looks out for the 9 inch drain hidden in the heather.

Draw.—Hounds that look for a fox are said to "draw" for it. Thus, to draw a covert is for the huntsman to persuade his hounds to look for a fox in it.

The draw, or the day's draw, is the area of the hunt's country in which it is proposed to look for foxes.

To draw a hound is (a) to draw it; (b) to separate it from the remainder of the pack. Thus, before drafting the hunting pack (see *Draft*) the huntsman draws each individual hound forming it from the rest of the pack.

Draw-yard.—That part of the kennels into which all the courts open, and from which the hounds are drawn by the huntsman before being fed.

Drench.—To drench a horse or hound is forceably to pour liquid—probably medicine or stimulant—down its neck from a bottle or drenching-horn.

Drop-fence.—Is a fence of which the ground on the landing side is lower than the ground on the take-off side.

Droppings.—The excreta, or dung, of horses.

Dry single.—A bank without a ditch.

Dung.—the excreta, or droppings, of horses.

Dumping.—Dumping is a fault in the shoeing of horses, consisting of the rasping away of the front of the toe of the wall of the foot of the horse, either to shorten the toe, or to make the foot fit the shoe. If the toe does need shortening it should be rasped on the ground surface.

E

Enter.—To enter a hound is to teach it to hunt a fox. Unentered hounds are therefore hounds, probably, but not of necessity, puppies, which have never been taught to hunt a fox. Unentered hounds automatically become entered hounds on the day of the Opening Meet; for the remainder of that season they become "First Season" hounds.

F

Feather.—A hound may own a very weak scent but be uncertain that he *does* own it. In that case, he will snuffle along the line, his stern lashing from side to side, but he will not throw his tongue. He is feathering along the line.

Feathers.—A hound's feathers are the ruffled, long, hairs on the under-side of the lower part of his stern.

Field.—The collection of mounted men and women hunting with a pack; the hunt servants and second-horseman are not members of the field.

Field Boots.—All-brown long-boots.

Flags.—The flooring of the kennel-courts is known as the flags. Thus, to see a pack "on the flags" as opposed to seeing them "in the field" is to see them in kennels.

Flesh.—The meat—cow, horse, sheep, goat, ass—eaten by hounds.

Flesh-cart.—The vehicle, horse or petrol-drawn, that fetches dead cows, horses, sheep, goats, and asses, from the death-bed to the kennels.

Flesh-hovel.—A building which, in the distance (but only in the distance) closely resembles a rustic summer-house, found at kennels. In it are dismembered and disembowelled those carcases more or less recently deceased, upon which the hounds are fed. As readers are doubtless aware, one of the principal functions of the London season is the visit to the Garth flesh-hovel after the last race on Ladies' Day at Epsom.

Flute-bit.—A bit, consisting of a hollow, perforated, tube placed in horses' mouths to prevent their wind-sucking and crib-biting.

Flying country.—A country divided principally by flying fences. (In Ireland all fences which are not jumped "on-and-off" are "flies"—*i.e.*, walls, timber, etc.)

Flying fences.—Fences which can be jumped from a gallop.

Foil.—A fox who "runs his foil" is doubling on his own tracks.

A smell which tends to disguise or obliterate the fox's scent trail is called "foil," *e.g.*, manure, natural or artificial; smoke from a couch-grass, fire; the smell of horses, hounds, human beings, cattle, sheep, pheasants, deer, porcupines, etc.

Foiled ground is ground which has been subjected to a scent, stronger to hounds than the foxscent. A covert in which hounds themselves have been hunting for a long time becomes "foiled"; a recently manured field is "foiled"; so is a field containing, or which has recently contained, stock or horses. Foil is the arch-enemy of the pack.

Fore-arm.—The portion of a horse's or a hound's leg above the knee but below the shoulder.

Frog.—The india-rubbery portion of the bottom of a horse's foot.

Frost nails.—Sharp-headed nails which are driven into a horse's shoes so as to give him a firmer foot-hold on frosty roads or greasy ground.

Fullered shoes.—Horse-shoes of which the ground surface is hollowed or grooved; in the groove, or fullering, sit the heads of the nails. Fullered shoes are usual for hunters.

G

Gall.—A gall is a sore caused by the friction of some portion of a horse's saddlery or clothing; *e.g.*, a girth-gall.

Gallop.—To describe a hunt as a "good gallop" is to imply that it was fast and probably fairly short; a "quick thing" is a very fast gallop; "a good hunt," a "nice hunt," a "good hound-hunt" are all longer and slower than a "good gallop."

Galvayne's mark.—A depression, on the outer side of the top corner incisor-tooth of a horse's mouth, by the length of which some indication may be reached as to a horse's age.

Geld.—To geld a male horse or hound is to de-sex it. A gelding is a de-sexed male horse.

Girth.—The long, wide, strap which passes round the horse's middle, attached at each end to the saddle—the belly-band, in other words, except that it doesn't go round the belly. The girth of a horse or a hound is the distance round its body just behind the elbows. A "good girth" is a comparatively great distance round this portion of its anatomy, and is a sign of staying power and good constitution.

Going.—The nature of the ground as it affects a horse's ability to gallop; *e.g.,* hard, heavy, deep, wet, or, (rarely) good.

Good head.—Hounds carry a good head when they are running hard on a broad front, instead of tailed out.

Grass yard.—A small wired-in paddock attached to kennels in which hounds can be turned loose to exercise themselves when the huntsman is too inebriated (known as "indisposed") to exercise them.

Gruel.—A soothing, warm, drink, for tired horses.

Guarantee.—The sum of money which a Hunt Committee guarantees to pay the Master annually towards the cost of upkeep of kennels, hounds, horses, salaries, etc.

H

Hack, a.—A hack is, theoretically, a horse whose primary function it is to convey its rider from place to place. In pre-motor days, hacks were used to convey fox-hunters to the meet at a fast pace—the gallop—while their hunters were taken on sedately by grooms. Nowadays, a hack is either a riding-school horse or a highly trained type of show-horse, conversant with the meanings of such terms as Piaffe, and Pouffe (which I am not).

A hack-hunter (*vide* advertisements of horses for sale) is a four-legged animal, formerly like a horse in appearance, but now too old and too unsound to be used for any known equine function save that of feeding hounds.

Hack On, to.—To hack on to a meet is for the fox-hunter to ride on a horse to the meet.

Hackles.—The hackles of a hound are the hairs along the ridge of its spine (sometimes known in the West as the "ridge-hairs"). A hound that is angry "gets its hackles up," or, in other words, is all het up.

Hairy.—A hairy fence is one which is not clean-cut, but which is straggly and probably high; a hairy country is one abounding in such hairy fences.

Hands.—A horseman is said to possess "good hands" when he rides a horse with understanding and sympathy, and when his firm seat and delicate sense of touch enables him to control the horse with the minimum of pressure on the reins.

Hare foot.—A long hare-like foot, as opposed to a short, cat-like foot (of a hound). A hare foot is considered by those in the know as a serious fault of conformation.

Hay-net, a.—Bag-net into which a horse's ration of hay is stuffed and which is then hung in his box; it is made of stout string, and saves much waste.

Head, to.—To head a fox is to divert it from its original course.

Headland.—The edge of a field, near the hedge. Of a ploughed field, the uncultivated rim near the fence. The head-land is always the soundest part of a wet field.

Heads up.—Hounds are said to have their heads up when they no longer have their noses to the ground searching for the fox-scent.

Heel.—Hounds run heel, or "run the heel-way" when they follow the line of a fox in the opposite way to that in which he was travelling.

Hen-coop.—In some much-wired countries, a wooden "apron"—a wooden inverted V, which is thrown over a wire fence.

Hireling.—A horse which is let out on hire.

Hip-down.—A fracture of one of the bones of the hip of a horse, frequently caused by either falling on the road or being knocked against a stable door-post.

Hit, to make a.—May mean one of two things: in breeding, to found a successful line; in the hunting-field, to strike the line of the fox.

Hit the line.—A hound "hits" the line of the fox when he first smells it after a check; so too, a huntsman "hits" it when he causes a hound or hounds to strike it after a check.

Hock.—The elbow-like joint of a horse or a hound's hind-leg.

Hog.—The bristles of a horse's mane; hogging is the process of clipping the bristles shorter.

Hold.—A covert that contains a fox is said to "hold." To "hold" hounds on or round, or back, is to take them on, or round, or back.

Hold up.—To hold up a covert is to surround it and prevent foxes (as a rule, cubs) from leaving it. To "hold up" a litter (of cubs) is to surround the covert in which they live.

Hold up!—A term of endearment used to stumbling horses.

Holloa, a.—A scream, meaning the same as the spoken words "Tally-ho!"—that is, "I have seen a fox!" The words "Tally-ho!" are only used when they can be spoken—when the person for whom they are intended is within speaking distance; at long ranges, he is regaled with a holloa. Pronounced holler.

Hound Hunt.—See *Gallop*.

Hound pace.⎫—The pace at which horses jog when travelling
Hound jog. ⎭ with hounds on the road; about 6 m.p.h.

Huic!—Also written "Hoick!" Pronounced "Hike!" "Ike!" "Hark!" or "Ark!" Means Hark!

Huic Holloa!—Hark (to the) Holloa! A cheer drawing the attention of the huntsman or the hounds to a holloa.

Hunt.—To hunt: to pursue a quarry.

A hunt: the process of pursuing a quarry.

The hunt: the whole caboodle—men, women, hounds, horses, servants—that pursue a quarry. The organization of the hunt.

I

Irons.—Stirrup-irons: always known as "stirrup-irons" or "irons," never as "stirrups," in the best Meltonian circles.

J

Joint Masters.—Two or more individuals sharing the duties and burdens of the mastership of a hunt.

K

Kennel.—A fox's above-ground bed is his kennel; to unkennel him is to push him out of bed.

Kennels.—The abode of foxhounds.

Kennel-huntsman.—The individual, a professional hunt servant, who is in charge of the kennels. A professional huntsman is his own kennel-huntsman; where an amateur hunts the hounds it is usual for him to appoint a servant, probably his 1st whipper-in, to be in charge of the kennels: this is the kennel-huntsman.

Kennelman.—A servant who works in the kennels under the kennel-huntsman or huntsman, but who does not also take the field (*i.e.* a whipper-in may work in kennels, but he is not a kennelman).

Knee-caps.—Wool and leather protectors for the knees of horses.

L

Laminitis.—A cause of unsoundness in horses, being inflammation of the laminæ of the feet, or, if you are not much wiser, simply "fever in the feet."

Lark.—To lark over a fence is to jump it when hounds are not running, or on the way to or from hunting. It is a hunting field crime.

Leathers.—Of men, buckskin breeches. Of saddlery, stirrup leathers.

Lift.—A huntsman lifts hounds when he takes them, during the course of a hunt, across country without giving them time to try for the scent.

Ligament.—A ligament is attached to every joint, human and animal; its function is to prevent the joint being opened too wide.

Line, a.—The scent trail of a fox.

Linseed.—The seed of the flax. Known in Ireland and parts of England as "flackseed." Boiled, it is given as a fattener to horses.

Lipstrap.—A strap passing from one cheek of a bit to the other, through a link of the curb-chain; its function, a useful one, is to prevent the bit being reversed by a sudden jerk of the horse's head, or by any other calamity.

Livery.—A livery is a uniform worn by a private servant—*e.g.* a second horseman, or a hunt servant, or a footman.

A livery-stable is a stable which will take in horses at livery—that is, at which horses are looked after by, or on behalf of, the livery-stable-keeper for the horse-owner, in return for payment. A livery stable does not of necessity let horses out on hire, though it generally does so.

Lodging-room.—A room at the kennels in which hounds sleep.

Lymphangitis.—Alias Weed, Big-leg, or Monday-morning Disease. An Equine malady, affecting one or both hind-legs, which swell alarmingly. Due possibly to over-feeding and under-exercising.

Lymphatics.—A system of tubes, human and animal, which carry the good things produced by the bowels to the heart.

M

Make a pack.—To "make a pack" is to count the hounds in it.

Mahogany.—The dark-brown colour of the tops of top boots, when they are a dark-brown colour. They are then known as "mahogany tops."

Mark.—When hounds hunt a fox's line up to an earth, in which the fox is taking refuge, and then scrabble and bay outside, they are said to "mark the fox to ground" or, simply, to mark. A false mark is when they mark at a hole in which there is in fact no fox.

Martingales.—Are strappy things, hung round or near horse's necks (equine, not liquid). Now buy a horsey book and find out the difference between Standing and Running martingales, and Irish martingales—the latter not being martingales at all.

Mash.—A mash, or bran mash, is a mess of pottage, comprising bran and water, and possibly other ingredients such as oats or linseed, given to horses after hunting and on Saturday nights, as well as at other times when the spirit moves the stud groom.

Mask, a.—A fox's head, dead or alive.

M.F.H.—Master, or Masters, of Foxhounds.

M.F.H.A.—Masters of Foxhounds Association; the governing body of Fox-hunting.

M.H.—Inferior bodies, being merely Masters of Hounds (unspecified—hare, deer, stag, otter, drag, &c., &c.)

Meet, the.—The place of assembling, and assemblage, of the hunt (which see) before hunting.

Midlands.—The, predominantly grass, and rather up-stage, countries situated in the heart of England.

Mixed Pack.—A pack comprising hounds of both sexes; care is taken to ensure that the party is strictly moral.

Mob.—The Intelligentsia's name for a Hunt (which see).
    To mob a fox is to hunt it without giving it a chance
    to escape—that is, to surround it, or gallop after it.

Moss litter.—A form of bedding for horses made of broken-
    up peat.

Music.—The cry of hounds is also "the music of the pack,"
    or, more prosaically, hound-music.

Mute.—A hound runs mute when he follows the scent of a
    fox without throwing his tongue; a hound is mute when
    he never throws his tongue.

Muzzle.—The sharp end of a horse or a hound: comprises
    the nose, nostrils, and mouth.

N

Nappy.—A horse is said to be nappy when it refuses to jump
    or, more commonly, when it fights to go back to its
    stable.

Navicular.—A form of equine unsoundness, being inflamma-
    tion of the navicular bone of the foot.

Neck-cloth.—If you hear a real doggy sort of man complain
    that a hound "has plenty of neck cloth, eh?" he means
    that it is a "bit throaty, eh?"; in other words that the
    line of its throat is not clean; to be "throaty" is but to
    give offence to the well-trained eye—throatiness is not
    a working fault: indeed, some say that plenty of neck
    cloth means plenty of music.

Nerve.—To the fox-hunter, the opposite of nerves. Nerve is
    fox-hunting courage—ability to cross a country without
    for ever seeing visions and dreaming dreams of broken
    bones and split heads. Nerve cannot be purchased at
    12s. 6d. a bottle.

Nose.—The smelling-power of a hound. A hound with a
    good nose has good smelling power, plus the mental
    ability to interpret what he smells in terms of the fox's
    actual movements.

Nose-band.—Part of a horse's hunting-field apparel, being the
    broad leather band that circumnavigates his face just

below—two fingers below, to be accurate—the cheek-bone. It is now more fashionable for the fox-hunter to appear without breeches than for his horse to appear without a nose-band. But, unless a standing martingale is attached to it, it is an utterly useless garment: but then, so, really, are breeches.

O

Open.—The hound which, winding a fox in covert, is the first to speak to it, is said to "open."

An unstopped fox-earth is said to be "open."

Opening Meet.—The first meet of the regular hunting season. In theory, the hunting season starts on November 1st, but in practice the Opening Meet is held the first convenient day after that date, and may be delayed on account of the state of the ground, the condition of the fox-supply, or any other reason which to the Master may appear good. The Opening Meet is the first occasion on which the field appears in full dress. It is also, in many countries, the first day upon which strangers and non-subscribers are capped, though nowadays, in a few countries, a cap is taken during October.

Over at the knee.—The opposite to "back at the knee": *i.e.* a horse or hound is over at the knee when the fore-arm is in a vertical plane behind the leg below the knee.

Over-reach.—An injury to a horse's fore-leg caused by its being struck and bruised or cut, or bruised and cut, by the toe of the corresponding hind shoe; this generally occurs when landing over a fence or when suddenly galloping into soft ground, and is due to the horse being unable to extract his fore-foot in time for the arrival of his hind-foot. Some horses are more prone to over-reach than others.

Over-ride.—To over-ride is to ride too close to the Pack, and to give them insufficient freedom in which to hunt properly.

Over-shot.—Of a hound, the opposite of "swine chopped":

when the upper jaw protrudes beyond the lower—a fault of conformation.

Own the line.—A hound which is hunting on the fox's line is said to "own the line."

Oxer.—An ox-fence, consisting of a thorn fence protected on one side by a rail, standing some 3′ high and perhaps 3′ from it: a double oxer is a thorn fence with an ox rail on both sides.

P

Pack.—A collection of hounds.

Pad.—The foot of a fox: to pad a fox is to follow him, maybe only a few inches, by his pad-marks.

Panel.—The pad which covers the tree of a saddle. A jumping-place, specially made for the benefit of the hunt, in a fence.

Peck.—A horse is said to peck when, on landing over a fence, he falls on to his nose or his knees, but does not actually fall down. The "popular press" terms this "stumble over a hedge."

Pelham.—A bit, consisting of mouthpiece and cheeks, and so designed as to provide in one bit the functions of both snaffle and curb bits. It has two reins and a curb-chain.

"Peterborough."—Peterborough Royal Foxhound Show.

Pick up.—A huntsman is said to "pick hounds up" when he lifts them. See *Lift.*

Pillar reins.—These are used to secure a saddled or harnessed horse in his stall until he is needed. They consist of two long straps, attached at one end to the stall-post, and at the other, by means of a spring clip, to the horse's bit. He thus faces "outwards" in the stall and, though able to move his quarters cannot move his head. Probably, the past tense is more applicable to pillar reins since, with the passing of harness horses, and stalls, they are now rarely seen.

Pink.—Some people call a red, or scarlet, coat a "pink" coat; others, even, speak of hunting in pink, when they mean a scarlet, or red, coat, white breeches, &c.; in this case the one word "pink" covers a multitude of items of clothing. But the expression "pink" for scarlet or red is distinctly Edwardian musical-comedy-ish; probably "red" is the correct colour of a hunting coat, though "scarlet" is quite legitimate. But you cannot use either in the sense "he hunts in red"—it must be "he hunts in a red coat."

Pipe.—A branch-hole of a fox or rabbit earth is termed a "pipe."

Plate.—The super-horsey, among whom are fortunately numbered but few fox-hunters, are apt to talk of "the plate" when they mean "the saddle"—why, goodness knows.

A plate is also a perfectly legitimate and un-horsey term for a very light racing shoe, and to "plate" a horse is to fit it with such shoes.

Plough.—Arable country is always called "plough" by the fox-hunter; an arable field is "plough" or "ploughland" or "a field of plough" even though it may in actual fact be growing a crop at the time. The arable parts of the East of England are frequently spoken of as "the ploughs."

Point.—The point of a run is the distance between the two farthest-apart points of it, measured as the crow flies; it is not, of necessity, the distance between find and finish, which might be nil while the point was 6 miles.

Port.—The port of a bit is the hoop-like affair sticking up from the middle of the bar. Its principal function is to prevent the tongue from taking the pressure of the bit off the bars, upon which it is supposed to act. It should not be so high as to act as a lever upon the roof of the mouth.

Poultry Fund.—A fund maintained by the hunt from which to pay compensation to poultry-owners for the loss of birds taken by foxes. Only those birds taken during the daytime or from reasonably fox-proof runs during the night are usually paid for, it being considered reasonable to expect poultry-owners to shut their birds up at night.

Pressure bandage.—Is used on the leg of a horse for the treatment of sprains or the reduction of "soft" enlargements.

Prick.— To prick a horse is to run a horse-shoe nail into the sensitive part of its foot, instead of, as intended, into the insensitive part.

Private Pack.—A pack of hounds maintained by the Master without the assistance of subscriptions. A private pack may, and often does, expect a subscription or donation to a damage, wire, or poultry fund, but the Master receives no assistance towards his "kennel expenses."

Provinces.—All hunting countries of England, Wales, and Scotland except the five Shire countries.

Pudding.—Oatmeal porridge as fed to hounds.

Puer.—Hound-dung.

Put down.—Of hounds and horses, to "destroy" on account of age or infirmity or accident.

Put to.—To stop a fox earth on the morning of a hunting day with the idea of keeping any fox already inside, and of preventing a hunted fox getting inside.

Pye.—A foxhound colour, lighter than tan; there are a variety of pyes—Lemon, Hare, and Badger.

Q

Quick Thing.—A very fast, short, gallop.

R

Rasper.—A very big fence.

Rate.—To rate a hound is to "correct it by the voice for any act of ill-discipline" according to the Lonsdale Library *Fox-hunting.* That is, in plainer English, to blast it.

Ride.—A ride is a wide path through a covert.

Ring, the.—The ring is the show-ring.

Ringbone.—A cause of equine unsoundness, being ossification of the cartilage of a foot.

Ringing.—A ringing fox is a fox that runs in circles, never going far from where it was found.

Ringworm.—A skin disease.

Riot.—Anything, from the proverbial cat in a kitchen to a wagtail in the wallflowers, which hounds hunt when they should only hunt fox. To riot is to hunt these other anythings: they include rabbits, hares, deer, pheasants, moorhens, cats and cur-dogs—in fact, everything which moves.

Rogue.—A rogue is a vicious horse; a merely playful horse is not a rogue, even though it may, while "playing" behave exactly as does the rogue. A rogue *means* it—"it" varying from biting in the stable to rubbing against apple-trees outside.

Roller.—The surcingle used to keep a horse-rug on the horse.

Roots.—Root-crops—turnips, swedes, beet, mangolds, potatoes, &c. Cabbages and kale are *not* roots.

Rough country.—A country that is difficult to ride over, even to one of unblemished nerve and capabilities. That is to say, a hilly country, a wooded country, a moorland country, and so on.

Roughing.—A comprehensive term for preparing the horse's shoes to cope with slippery roads: roughing includes fitting frost cogs and frost-nails.

Rounding.—Cutting off the points of hounds' ears, making them round instead of pointed. This is done, for the sake of foolish fashion, when they are puppies; it is fast going out of fashion. And quite right too.

Rubber.—A stable rubber is a horse-duster.

Running.—Hounds are said to be running when they are in actual pursuit of a fox. Thus, though they may be galloping to go to a holloa they are not technically running: but they are technically running when they are only walking after a fox on a very cold scent. They are not running when they are drawing or checked.

S

Sandcrack.—An equine infirmity, being a fissure of the horn of the wall of the foot of the horse.

Scarlet.—A legitimate name for the colour of a red hunting-coat. See also *Pink*.

Screw, a.—A screw is a cheap, probably unsound, horse. The horses belonging to the fox-hunter's friends are always screws; his own, never.

Seated Shoes.—A horse-shoe of which the bearing surface is less than the ground surface, used for horses with very flat soles.

Shelly.—A hound is shelly when his body is weak and wasp-waisted; weedy.

Shires.—The area covered by the five Shire Packs: Pytchley, Quorn, Fernie's, Cottesmore, and Belvoir.

Single bank.—A bank with a ditch on only one side.

Sinking.—A fox is said to be sinking when he is getting weaker, towards the end of a hunt.

Skirt.—A hound which does not follow the true line of the fox, but cuts off corners, and a fox-hunter who does not follow the true line of the pack (and so of the fox) but cuts off corners, both "skirt" and are "skirters."

Speak.—Fox-hounds do not "bark"; they "speak," which, of course, is far more genteel.

Splint.—An equine calamity, being a small bony nob sprouting out of a cannon bone and causing the value of the horse to drop considerably; causes lameness when knocked and when forming.

Stableman.—A man who works in stables under a groom.

Stain.—Foil, which see.

Stake-and-bound.—Nearly, but not quite, a cut-and-laid fence.

Stale line.—The line of a fox which has been gone a long time and of which the scent is almost non-existent.

Stallion.—A he-horse.

Stallion-hound.—A he-hound.

Stern.—Foxhounds do not have tails, only sterns.

Stopping.—Or stopping out. Fox earths are "stopped" when

they are blocked during the hours of darkness preceding a hunting-day. The fox is then out, and the object of the manœuvre is to make him sleep out next day and so be available for hounds to find. Compare with *Putting to.*

Stub-bred.—Foxes which are born above ground are called stub-bred. They are commonly supposed to be hardier and stronger.

Stud.—A collection of horses; a collection of horses kept for breeding purposes—*i.e.* of he-horses and she-horses, together with their progeny; frost-cogs and frost-nails are also sometimes spoken of as "studs."

Stud-groom.—A groom in charge of a stable of horses, or of a stud-farm.

Strapper.—A man who works in stables under a groom.

Swine-chopped.—A hound is swine-chopped when his lower jaw protrudes beyond his upper jaw.

T

Tail-hounds.—Hounds which, in a hunt, are some way behind the main body of the pack.

Tally-Ho!—A hunting-cry meaning "I have seen a fox!" See *Holloa!*

Tally-over!—A hunting-cry, meaning "I have seen a fox cross this ride (or road)."

Terrier-man.—A man employed by a hunt to lead or carry terriers.

Thoroughpin.—An equine unsoundness, being an enlargement in front of and above the hock.

Throaty.—See *Neck-cloth.*

Thrown out.—A fox-hunter is said to be thrown out when, for any cause, he loses his place in a hunt.

Thrush.—An equine complaint, being a smelly disease of the frog of the foot, caused by dirt and neglect.

Timber.—Post-and-rails, hunt jumps made of wood, gates—anything wooden and jumpable is known as "timber"; by the most horsey, the word "carpentry" is at times used.

Tongue.—The cry of hounds. To "throw the tongue" is to bark or "speak."

Tops.—Top-boots. Long black boots with a few inches of coloured top above the black; worn only with white breeches. Butcher boots, which are all-black, are not top-boots since they have no tops.

To Touch the horn.—To blow the horn.

Tread.—An injury to the coronet caused by the other fore, or hind, foot; of horses, of course.

Trencher fed.—A pack which is trencher fed is kept, by ones and twos, among the farmers, &c., of the neighbourhood, and are collected together on a hunting-morning. There are very few trencher-fed packs left now.

U

Unentered hounds.—Are hounds which have not yet learnt to recognize and follow the scent of a fox; normally, a hound which has not finished one cub-hunting season, but rarely one gets a hound which takes two or more cub-hunting seasons to learn to hunt: others learn all about it at walk.

V

Valeting-room.—A room at the kennels where the hunt servants' clothes and boots are cleaned.

Vices.—The vices of a hound are: skirting, babbling, rioting, running mute, refusing to draw.

The vices of a horse are: rearing, bucking, kicking, plunging, biting, lying down, running away, napping, shying, and jibbing. Stable vices are: biting, kicking, crib-biting, weaving, and windsucking, though the last three are really nervous diseases.

View.—To see a fox is to view it; the sight of a fox is a view.

View Holloa.—See *Holloa!*

Vixen.—A she-fox.

Voluntary.—To cut a voluntary is to fall off the horse. If you get a fall because the horse itself falls or pecks badly you do not "cut a voluntary."

W

Walk.—Foxhound puppies, for the good of their souls and bodies—not least, the former—are sent out to farms and private houses from the age of about 2–3 months to the age of about 9–12 months; they are then said to be "at walk"; the places at which they are thus temporarily domiciled are "walks," and the temporary custodians are "walkers."

Walking out.—Has nothing to do with "at walk" but is, unlike most fox-hunting expressions, what it says. Walking out is the act of taking the pack out for its hour's walking exercise, which it should receive twice daily.

Water-brush.—An equine grooming-brush used primarily for washing the feet; since it is composed of soft bristles it is also usefully employed in grooming ticklish and delicate portions of the equine anatomy, such as the face, &c.

Watering-bridle.—A bridle designed primarily for exercise—originally for taking horses to water. It consists of cheap leather and a galvanized iron snaffle bit. It is cheap, and will not seriously deteriorate from lack of cleaning.

Weaving.—A stable vice; the horse rocks from side to side in its stall, placing its weight first on one fore-foot, then on the other, the head and neck keeping time in lateral movements; it is a nervous complaint: in its treatment and eventual cure there is an obvious opening for an equine psychologist.

"Welsh."—Foxhounds are either pure English, pure Welsh, or English-Welsh cross bred. There are very few pure Welsh hounds in existence, but there are many crossbred English-Welsh. These generally have a great deal less than 5 per cent. of Welsh blood in their veins, yet they may display the rough coat typical of the pure Welsh, and may be—generally are—spoken of as being "Welsh" or "Welshmen."

Whelps.—Unweaned puppies.

Whin.—In some parts, especially the North of England, a gorse covert is called a whin.

Whip.—An instrument for the flagellation of horses and hounds (to say nothing of small boys) and the opening of gates. Not to be confused with "whipper-in."

Whipper-in.—An assistant to the huntsman in both kennel and field. Not to be confused with "Whip."

Whistle.—In some hunts a whistle is employed in place of a Holloa. In others the whistle is confined to the hunt horses; a whistling horse is one that, to all intents and purposes, is already slightly affected in the wind and which has every chance of becoming much more seriously affected in the very near future—at any rate, if you buy it.

White line.—A part of the equine foot, being the junction between the sensitive and insensitive laminæ; beyond the "white line" the shoeing smith must not drive a nail; if he does he will "prick" the horse.

Wind.—Of a hound, the act of smelling a fox is "winding a fox."

Of a horse, the respiratory processes: *e.g.* "gone in the wind" means "broken winded" or afflicted with diseased respiratory organs (the larynx).

Wind-sucking.—An equine stable vice, or nervous complaint, being the mother and father of crib-biting; in this case the horse swallows neat air without going to the trouble of biting the manger—he just swallows.

Wisping.—A branch of grooming. A wisp is a plaited handful of hay or straw, and whisping consists in banging this down on the more easily accessible portions of the horse's anatomy—(but not on the loins which might be damaged in the process): oddly enough, it is of great benefit to the horse, and in the best stables "wisping" takes place for 15 or 20 minutes every evening.

Woodland.—A very large covert is called a woodland.

Lightning Source UK Ltd.
Milton Keynes UK
UKOW050734121111

181951UK00001B/53/P